William Henry Green

Prophets and prophecy

A compilation from notes of the lectures before the senior class

William Henry Green

Prophets and prophecy
A compilation from notes of the lectures before the senior class

ISBN/EAN: 9783337274665

Printed in Europe, USA, Canada, Australia, Japan

Cover: Foto ©Lupo / pixelio.de

More available books at **www.hansebooks.com**

Prophets and Prophecy

BY

Prof. W. H. Green.

A COMPILATION FROM NOTES OF THE LECTURES
BEFORE THE SENIOR CLASS.

[PRINTED, NOT PUBLISHED.]

The Princeton Press
C. S. ROBINSON & CO., STEAM POWER PRINTERS
1895

THE PROPHET.

What is meant by the term "prophet" in the O. T.? True definition: An authoritative and infallible expounder of the will of God.

The books of the prophets form an important part of the O. T. writings. This importance is shown in four particulars:

1. *In their authority.*—They contain a divine revelation of God's will, and dealings with Israel through over four hundred years, which will is still binding, in its essence, on us to-day.

2. *In their historical value.*—They show to us the religion and theology of the theocracy in its doctrinal aspect, in its most advanced stages.

3. *In their Messianic value.*—They contain the fullest and clearest disclosures B. C. concerning the coming Redeemer, his work among men, and his ignominious death upon the cross. They give the criteria for his recognition, holding him up before the world as an object of faith and hope.

4. *In their apologetic value.*—They contain the most astonishing exhibitions of supernatural foresight in numerous predictions, whose fulfillment furnishes us with a powerful argument for the truth and divinity of our religion. In these four points the prophecies are most important.

For the study and appreciation of the character of the prophets, we must first see what is meant by the term prophet.

I. DEUTERONOMY 18: 18, 19.

The true idea of an O. T. prophet may be learned first and most explicitly from the formal definition given in Deut. 18: 18, 19: "I will raise them up a Prophet from among their brethren, like unto thee, and will put my words in his mouth; and he shall speak unto them all that I shall command him. And it shall come to pass, *that* whosoever will not harken unto my words which he shall speak in my name, I will require *it* of him." This passage is applied by Peter in Acts 3: 22, 23, to Christ, and is supposed by some to refer to Christ alone. The difficulty of this is found in the connection, which is two-fold:

a. There were no diviners, charmers, consulters, wizards or necromancers, Deut. 18: 9-14, to whom they were permitted to resort. The people were forbidden to use any other means of inquiring into the will of God, as the heathen had done, for they would have no need of it, for God would raise them up a prophet.

b. In condescension to the weakness of the people, as shown on Mount Sinai, when they were not able to endure the presence of God, he promises to send them a prophet, or to raise up one who should stand between them and God. Now so distant an event as Christ's coming could not be used as a reason for their not applying to diviners, or to some substitute for the God of heaven. There must be a nearer one than Christ, hence the O. T. prophet.

It is plain from the original language that this passage from Deut. 18: 18, 19, being the ground of two different applications, these two applications must be reconciled, by making Deut. 18: 18, 19, refer to the line of prophets, and that of Peter in Acts 3: 22, 23, must refer to Christ, the last and greatest of all the prophets. The passage has a Messianic reference, and therefore comprehends Christ and the O. T. prophets. We must conciliate this double reference.

Different Views of the Term "Prophet."—A. Some commentators take the word prophet in Deut. in a collective sense, *i. e.*, it is a singular noun used for the plural. *Answer* 1. This view is unreasonable, for nowhere else is a singular used for a plural. 2. To so use it, would destroy the individuality of the term, which is so marked, and, besides, all the verbs and pronouns are also used in the singular. B. Some apply it to Joshua, instead of taking it in a collective sense. On the whole, it seems best to understand it in its generic sense, as *Havernick*; or, in an ideal sense, as Hengstenberg, that is: *a.* Equivalent to a prophet at each time of emergency; *b.* Equivalent to a prophet, that is, a complex or ideal person, conceived of as a unit, but embracing in it a whole line, or order of prophets; *e. g.*, the Pope of Rome is an ideal man, he is one of many in the line of popes; the President of the United States is an ideal man, being one of many presidents. It is in this sense, that all are combined as one person, into an ideal unity. He argues—

1. That the prophetic order was to culminate in Christ.

2. Is called the "spirit of Christ," as in 1 Peter 1: 11, for the spirit of Christ was to speak through the prophets. In Peter it says, "searching what, or what manner of time the Spirit of Christ which was in them did signify when it testified beforehand the sufferings of Christ, and the glory that should follow." The Spirit of Christ spoke through these prophets; he therefore was, in a certain sense, the only prophet.

Essential Particulars.—*a*. God would put his words into his mouth.

b. Infallibility. He should speak to the people all things commanded, and should give it just as he received it.

c. His authority should be absolute and unconditional. To refuse or reject him was to refuse or reject God. This subject may still further be illustrated by Moses, thus placing the *prophets in contrast with two classes of men*.

1. *In contrast with heathen diviners*, v. 10; and with prophets who spake in the name of other gods, v. 20. These last thought, or sought, to penetrate the will of deity by the observation of omens. This is denounced and prohibited in the verses following.

2. *In contrast with false prophets*, who profess to speak in the Lord's name, but are unauthorized. These are to be distinguished by their uttering what does not come to pass, v. 22; and in teaching what is at variance with what God has taught them, Deut. 13: 1–5. These heathen diviners were of heathen origin, and introduced by heathen nations. They belong to the earlier stages, *i. e*., those under the first, and from the Canaanites, *e. g*., the "witch of En-dor." Or they belong to the apostate Kingdom of the ten tribes, "prophets of Baal," 1 Kings 18: The false prophets from Israel belonged to a later date, and to Judah. They were courted on account of their smooth words, Jer. 28: 15; 29: 8–9; Micah 3: 5.

II. NAMES, EPITHETS, ETC.

This is another source whence to derive a true idea of the prophet. They are—
1. Those names which describe them absolutely.
2. Those which describe them relatively to God.
3. Those which describe them relatively to the people.

נָבִיא　　*a. Nabhi:* common term applied to prophet.
רֹאֶה　　*b. Roeh:* A seer. And in Hosea 9:7, we have:
אִישׁ הָרוּחַ　*c. Ish haruahh:* Man of the spirit: inspired man (poetic).

1. Description Absolutely.—*Roeh:* Seer does not mean one who simply sees visions, as some have supposed, but one who possesses the power or faculty of foresight in a higher degree than ordinary men. Not confined to visions strictly, but in a wider sense to one who, by God's power, could see what lay hid to others; the hidden will of God. The common designation of prophets is *nabhi*, from *nabha*, to bubble forth; with the passive signification, is one on whom the spirit of the Lord is poured out, as given by some interpreters. But in Hebrew it signifies "dropping;" hence words significant of dropping, are figuratively referred to speaking; therefore, to speak, and in the passive sense one who is qualified to speak—one skilled in pouring forth meaning of the word is seen from Ex. 7:1, "I have made spring pour forth its waters." That this is the primary word—one who pours forth words or utterances, as "thee a god to Pharaoh, and Aaron, thy brother, shall be thy prophet," *i. e.*, his spokesman. Hence, what God says to Moses must mean, one who is a mouth-piece of God to man.

So also in the Greek, *prophets* is commonly interpreted as *pro*, beforehand, hence speaking beforehand. Again, in a local sense, to speak beforehand was only a subordinate function of the prophet, hence, *pro* has been referred to place and not to time, which is the primary signification.

Nabhi gives authority to declare the word of God. This gives signification to 1 Sam. 9:9. "Beforetime in Israel, when a man went to enquire of God, thus he spake, Come, and let us go to the seer: for *he that* is now *called* a Prophet was beforetime called a Seer." Prediction is only subordinate. *Pro*, in local sense, indicates one who speaks in the presence of another for him; seer describes simply one who sees; while prophet is one who speaks what he sees.

2. Description Relatively to God.—The second series of names are those which show their relation to God, *e. g.*, 1 Sam. 2:27, "And there came a man of God unto Eli." Again, they are called servants, 2 Kings 17:23, "As he had said by all his servants the prophets." They are called messengers, 2 Chron. 36:15, 16, "They wait upon Him ready to do His bidding." These terms, from their nature, are inapplicable to those in the service of false gods. They have, however, a wider sense, a more general use, and are not restricted to prophets, but are used of any employed by God to do his work. Jer. 25: 9, "Nebuchadnezzar, the king of Babylon, my servant." The angels, also, are his messengers, Ps. 119: 91, "For all are thy servants."

3. **Description Relatively to Man.**—Thus they are called *Roeh:* shepherds, signifying their duty to protect, guide and feed the flock of God. The general term applied to civil rulers and priests. They are called watchmen, interpreters. The word watchman is equivalent to two Hebrew words, one derived from *aphah*, to set at a distance, to watch, Is. 21: 6, "Go, set a watchman." *Shamar:* a guardian set in the streets or on the walls, a watchman to guard near at hand, to sound the alarm, Is. 62: 6. Interpreters: those who explain the otherwise unintelligible will of God. He imparts utterances of God's will, Is. 43: 27. These words correspond to seer and prophet in order. The watchman is one who sees what others do not. A seer is a supernatural watchman. An interpreter utters clearly God's will as a prophet. His qualifications for the functions of a prophet are divine, hence, what he utters is inspired.

III. PHRASES AND EXPRESSIONS.

We gather the true idea of a prophet by collecting and comparing the various phrases and expressions about them. That God's will is made known to them is seen:

1. Because God speaks to them, He shows them what to say, and what to do; His spirit rests upon them; His words come to them; they hear Him, hence revelations are made to them, and "thus saith the Lord" shows a divine communication.

2. That they are commissioned to declare His will is also asserted, *e. g.*, God sends them, bids them prophesy, gives them tongues to speak. They are charged with authoritative communications to others. They are bound to deliver these under the severest penalties. They declare what they have from God, in contrast with false prophets. They always preface what they say with, "Thus saith the Lord." So completely is the prophet's own personality lost that often the pronoun is changed, as if God spoke directly. Divine impartation of divine instruction. Modern critics say it is merely a mode of expression among the people, and not actual in fact.

Skeptical Opinions.—1. Some regard the prophets as men of superior enlightenment dealing with ignorant people. To conciliate favor for their utterances they publish them as coming from the deity, i. e., impostors.

2. Others say the prophets were the most advanced representatives of public sentiment. Enthusiasm thus referred to God. They combined what was in the popular heart. They were men who enthusiastically thought that all this was inspirations, i. e., enthusiasts.

3. The prophets, they say, were really inspired of God, but only as every right exercise of our faculties is under God's guidance. They differ from Christians not in kind, but in degree. Taking any one of these cases, and adopt their views, it takes away the grand distinction of a prophet, it robs them of their spiritual and scriptural meaning.

ANSWER (1). The supernatural character of the prophet is involved in the supernatural character of the O. T., and of religion in general.

(2). Though the prophets were holy men, and many of them were highly gifted, yet the inspiration was distinct from their sanctification. Even men who were destitute of piety were thus inspired,—Balaam, Saul, Caiaphas.

(3). It appears from the nature of these communications made to the prophets, that they were such as necessarily imply supernatural communications from above.

(4). It is universally conceded, even by skeptics, that while other nations had their oracles, etc., yet the prophets of Israel stood alone in the character of their revelations. There were deep thinkers elsewhere, and philosophers, but they do not rise beyond ambiguous responses. If prophecy is inherent in all men, how is it that the prophets of Israel stand alone in the purity, value and fitness of their communications.

4. Another limitation of the term prophet, not by skeptics, but by religious people, is that a prophet refers to one who foretells future events. The Fathers also held this view. The error is in mistaking a part for the whole of their duty, and the means for the end. Foretelling the future, was of course, important, yet it held a subordinate place. The prospective nature of their work gave it a prophetic character. They were not predicters merely, but also teachers, although this, in a large measure, came to overshadow the rest. The constant aim of these disclosures is lost sight of, beside their own inherent grandeur. Remark.

1. There is no specific reference to future events found in any one of the definitions of prophet already given. However conspicuous this element may appear, it is not essential to the office. They were to speak all that was commanded them, whether present, past or future.

2. In actual fact we see that the revelations of the prophets do not concern the future exclusively, but refer to the past and present as well, e. g., when Samuel told Saul that his father's asses had been found, 1 Sam. 9 : 20, this is past. Ahijah, though blind, yet knew and prophesied to Jeroboam's wife, when she came to him in his old age, 1 Kings 14 : 6–16. This shows present power. Elisha told Gehazi where he had been, 2 Kings 5 : 26. Daniel related a dream of Nebuchadnezzar, Dan. 2 : 28. Elisha told the King of Israel words spoken in the bed-chamber by the Syrian king's servant, 2 Kings 6 : 12. Ezekiel 24 : 2, tells them the very day, "Even of this same day the king of Babylon set himself against Jerusalem."

3. The function of the Hebrew prophet was not limited to the revealing of secret events. This was not the main and characteristic part of their work. They were principally divinely instructed guides, and the instructors of the people. They maintained in its dignity and integrity the covenant relation of the people with God. This was their particular function, and to conduct the people towards the end for which that relation was established, i. e., the coming of Christ, and his great salvation. His future purposes were revealed, as were also the past and the present.

4. To regard the predictions or prophecies merely in the light of prediction of divine help is to mistake entirely their grand aim. This would exalt the subordinate end over the principal. The evidence was often incomplete until the fulfillment, and hence many would thus lose their meaning and value, for the prophets were contemporaries. Other prophecies are considered doubtful, because obscure and enigmatical. Others still by the failure of God to preserve authentic records. Many prophecies were not compiled in the time of the prophets.

DEUTERONOMY 18 : 18. *It adds two other functions of the prophets.*

1. They were invariably of the chosen people. Balaam though a foreigner, was no exception to the rule, for the name prophet is given to him only in the N. T. (2 Peter 2; 16), and here it is used in its wider, more general sense.

Balaam is nowhere called a prophet in the O. T. but in Joshua 13, 22, he is called a soothsayer, and in Num. 22: 7, " rewards of divination " He was summoned as a soothsayer; God made use of him as he did of the witch of Endor, but this did not constitute him one of the prophets. So also he made use of Abimelech concerning Abraham's wife, Gen. 20:3. To this may be added Pharoah's dream, Gen. 41:1. Also Nebuchadnezzar's dream, Dan. 2:1. These are revelations. The dream of the man in the host of Midian, Judges 17: 13, 14. All these were for the benefit of God's chosen people, and were confined to the extraordinary circumstances which evoked them, but none of these were prophets.

2. A second particular in this passage of Deuteronomy is that the prophet was to be one like unto Moses; that is, the revelations made to him would be like those made unto Moses, a continuation of the scheme which he had begun, and in the same spirit. They were not therefore isolated phenomena, but vital relations to the former scheme. All belonged to one closely related scheme, initiated by Moses, and to be continued by them in likeness to him. The revelation of the O. T. is one, a regular unfolding begun by Moses, and carried on by succeeding prophets: their teachings must be like his, and built upon his. The prophets were not antagonistic to the law, but contemplated by the law itself, not to reform it, but to keep it before the minds of the people. It was no afterthought to meet an emergency, but provided for by Moses. It was opposed to false glosses put upon the law, and to those who sheltered themselves behind the law. So Christ was also against tradition. Ezekiel 18: 20, is not opposed to Exodus 20: 5. This is not contradictory. He, while claiming that they suffered for their fathers' sins, says they also suffered for their own, and putting false constructions on the law, Exodus says, " of them that hate me." Ezekiel appeals to Deut. 24: 16. Therefore, Ezekiel is the same as Moses, and contrary to false interpretations. They base their instruction on the law, and so always enforce it. This oneness of the prophets with the law, is repeatedly recognized in the O. T., as well as in the N. T., Is. 1: 11–14. The prophet here is showing the worthlessness of the ceremony, and does not aim at the abolition of the ritual, but rebukes their heartless formality, joined with ungodly living. Sacrifices became unendurable when joined with lives of sin. The

prophets were divinely commissioned reformers, not of the law, but of the people. The law needed no correction. They repeat and re-enact the law. Allusions to it abound everywhere, and all their instructions are based upon the law. Is. 8: 20, refers to the law and testimony. Mal. 4: 4. Though no direct citations, yet as we see allusions are everywhere found in the prophets, even the forms of expression show familiarity with the law. The law and the prophets are combined in the O. T., *e. g.*, Zech. 7: 12. So in the N. T. we find the expressions, "Moses and the prophets," "the law and the prophets."

From the preceding, we see that the prophet is—

1. Favored with the immediate dislosure of the divine will.

2. He is authorized to make it known.

3. Inspired in recording and teaching it.

We now come to consider, with additional clearness, not only absolutely, but relatively, *their position in the theocracy and in the great scheme of divine revelation.*

1. As to certain orders the question arises, How do the prophets stand related to other contemporaneous orders of men? We inquire in the general scheme of divine revelation.

2. As to other subsequent and antecedent modes of divine communication.

Priests.—The priests were a sacred order of men, mediators between God and man. The radical difference is— The priests acted on the part of man before God; the prophets on the part of God before man. The priests were such by hereditary descent, from representative tribes and families. The levites were selected as representatives for the rest of the people. The priests were an organized body, with gradations of rank. Levites, the priests, and then High Priest. They carried the principle of representation to its farthest extent. The high-priest was highest in rank. They were supported by a legal income, from the people in whose behalf they acted. In other ancient nations, as Egypt, the prophets belonged to the priesthood, but it was not so in Israel.

The prophets were without any regular succession. They had no organization among them; no stipend. They were called to the office by the immediate agency of the Spirit of God, by His sovereign pleasure. They might be taken from any tribe, not excepting Levi, *e. g.*, Samuel, 2 Chron. 20: 14.

They might come from any part of the land, even from Galilee, as Nahum and Jonah, notwithstanding the sneer: "There ariseth no prophet out of Galilee;" John 7: 52. They might and did come from any rank. Royal blood, *c. g.*, Isaiah, Daniel, Zephaniah. Or from priestly rank, Zechariah, Jeremiah, Ezekiel. Or from the most obscure herdsmen, as Amos. They might be taken from either sex, as Miriam the prophetess Ex. 15: 20; Deborah, Judges 4: 4; Huldah, 2 Chron. 34: 22; Anna, Luke 2: 26; and four daughters of Philip, Acts 21: 9. Their descent from the prophets was not essential, nor the contrary, 2 Chron. 15: 18. Azariah, also Jehu, 2 Chron. 19: 2 and other cases. It belonged to the prophets to declare the will of God. They were valued as being inspired of God. The priests were not usually inspired, their province being to offer sacrifices for the people before God, and to obtain for them the forgiveness of sins, and yet in consequence of the mediatorial character belonging to these two classes, the functions sometimes overlapped. The priests were authoritative expounders of the divine will. In the early period especially was this true, as Joshua in Num. 27: 21; Deut. 33: 8–10. Repeated mention is made of consultation, I Sam. 14: 3; I Sam. 22: 13; Judges 18: 5. Degenerate Priests asked counsel of God no doubt in imitation of true method of procedure.

While the prophets were permanent, and the priests not so much so, yet in Ezra 2: 63, they are commanded not "to eat of the most holy things till there stood up a priest with Urim and Thummim." And in John 11: 51, the high-priest prophesied of Christ's death. In regard to immediate divine communication there is this distinction: the prophet received his knowledge by the direct illumination of the Holy Spirit, while the priest received his knowledge from Urim and Thummim, or the ephod belonging to it. The difference between them may be illustrated by the heathen oracles as opposed to augurs who consulted omens and entrails of animals. Beside the supernatural responses, it was the ordinary province of the priest to teach the law to the people, and to deliver the will of God to them in doubtful cases, Lev. 10: 10; Haggai 2: 11. The prophets were to intercede for the people only by the free offering of prayer; the priests by symbolical ritual, Lev. 10: 3; Deut. 33: 10.

Judges.—Another sacred order of men were the judges—extraordinary judges. They, like prophets, were the immediate representatives of God, hence they were called to their office by the direct agency of the Holy Spirit. They were limited to no particular tribe, family, rank, occupation, sex. Deborah was a judge as well as a prophet; Judges 6: 4. Like the prophets, they were inspired, were under the immediate guidance of the Holy Spirit, but for different purposes. They were not to teach, but to rule. They were fitted for the special duties of their office. The office of judge was executive and administrative. They were extraordinary magistrates and leaders raised up by God himself in time of special need. They may be called divinely appointed dictators. The prophets were divinely inspired teachers, or expounders of the will of God, but exercised none of the functions of the magistracy. Their aims were not political. Their words are not to be viewed in a political or patriotic aspect. We do occasionally find them confronting kings, but they do not on this account deserve to be esteemed as tribunes of the people or guardians of public liberty. Elijah came into repeated conflicts with Ahab; Elisha sent a youth to anoint Jehu as king of Israel and destroyer of the house of Ahab. Hosea and Isaiah denounced the dangerous alliance of the kings with Assyria and Egypt. Jeremiah was also against Zedekiah. In all these cases they acted as teachers from God, not as politicians, but as religious instructors. They did not seek the office, and were not building up a political party; they were not demagogues. What they opposed was not on the ground of impolicy, but sin. What they maintained was for the honor and the law of God. We must bear in mind that the government of Israel differed from all others. In the true sense it was a theocracy, not by ecclesiastics, by priests, but by God himself. It was government by the direct manifestation of God's will. He gave them law, appointed their rulers; they were his vicegerents, and hence this gave a religious complexion to all the affairs of state. The idolatry of Ahab's house was a violation of the constitution of Israel, as the covenant people of God, and so often called for the intervention of the prophets. Alliances with heathen nations were crimes against the government of Israel, and the will of God. The evils which the prophets predicted were held up as the just judgments of God. When the prophets were consulted by kings and rulers, the responses were not dictated by policy, but by the divine will.

While the prophets were such, and while they stand side by side with the priests and judges, and had their own proper work, yet their powers were limited only by their great commission from God. Their office might be so extended as to comprehend all the others. The prophets performed any functions that the occasion might demand. So, in cases of emergency, they might act either as priests, judges or rulers. It was not a profance intrusion for a prophet to offer sacrifices, as it would be for any one else, *e. g.*, in the days of the degeneracy of Saul. Here the prophets assumed the functions of priest. Samuel, though not a priest, yet offered sacrifices by virtue of his right as an immediate messenger of God. So also of Elijah and Elisha, 1 Sam. 13 : 8; 1 Kings 18 : 30. The ordinary officers had abdicated, or had been deposed. Elijah sacrificed at Carmel. Bread of the first-fruits was brought to Elisha, which he was commanded to give to the hungry people, 2 Kings 4 : 42. These fruits were due to the priests. The people resorted to Elisha at new-moons, and on the Sabbath, etc., 2 Kings 4 : 23. Samuel took supreme direction over the commonwealth, and acting as judge anointed Saul king, 1 Sam. 7 : 15. He subsequently deposed him and appointed David. Ahijah prophesies to Jeroboam, 1 Kings 11 : 29. Elijah was directed to anoint Hazael king over Syria, and Jehu king over Israel, 1 Kings 19 : 15, 16; 2 Kings 8 : 12, 13. Not only did they depose and set up rulers over the people of God, but over heathen states as well, being the ambassadors of that God who is ruler and supreme governor of the universe.

2. It only remains now to examine **the position of the prophets among the methods of divine communication.** There is a growing nearness and fullness. There is a difference in the modes of God's revelations of himself. By the first method, we have :

1. *The Theophany*, characteristic of the patriarchal period. God made himself personally known. He spoke in audible voice to Abraham concerning the offering up of his son Isaac; to Jacob, Abimelech and Laban in dreams. He appeared in human form to Abraham in the plains of Mamre, face to face. Then God needed no agent. But when the flood came, and the destruction of Sodom and Gomorrah, God himself declared it, and sent them out.

2. *Prophetic Stage.*—When the seed of the patriarchs swelled into a nation, a new mode of revelation was needed and supplied. The will of God was now revealed through prophets, especially Moses. God no longer stood aloof from and out of connection with men, so to speak. Divine virtue

was now made resident in particular men. The spirit descended upon them, and made them the depositaries of His will; Amos 3: 7, "He revealeth His secrets unto His servants the prophets." In the solemn transactions at Sinai, when the covenant of God was to be made between Him and His people, He spoke once more with His own voice, but all further communications were made through Moses, and the prophets raised up like to him. Miracles were wrought, and revelations made through them, e. g., the plagues of Egypt were sent and removed at the bidding of Moses. So, also, the Red Sea was divided at the uplifting of his rod. At his word the manna came down from heaven, and water gushed forth from the flinty rock for the famishing people. The drought came and disappeared at the bidding of Elijah. Sennacherib was not destroyed until Isaiah had first foretold it. This second mode or stage of revelation, while an advance on the theophany, was not the ultimate and highest, for Paul says in 1 Cor. 13: 8–10, "But whether there be prophecies, they shall fail; whether there be tongues, they shall cease; whether there be knowledge, it shall vanish away." Thus he shows that prophecy was preparatory to and emblematic of the future.

3. *The prophetic idea is realized* in two forms; *a*. Individual; *b*. Universal. All these gifts, etc., of prophets in the O. T. are but types of better things to come.

a. Individual. The prophetic idea found its consummation in the person of Christ. He was the prophet of God in the highest sense, Deut. 18: 18; Is. 42: 1; 49: 1; 61: 1. God no longer acts remotely; He no longer speaks from heaven, nor through His servants, but comes Himself as a man to instruct and bless His people. The prophets were thus types of Christ. The ladder which Jacob saw reaching down from heaven to earth, is thus fully realized.

b. Universal realizations. The idea of the prophets was destined also to be universally realized in the entire body of the people of God. The prophets belonged to the people. They had no native gifts of divination; they did not exercise their gifts for their own benefit, but for the good of the people at large. They were established among the people for the people. The spirit of prophecy belonged not to the prophets alone, but to all Israel, but was restricted to one individual at first, *e. g.*, Num. 11: 29, "Enviest thou for my sake? Would God that all the Lord's people were prophets, and that the Lord would put His spirit upon them!" When Moses desired in this passage that all the people might become prophets, he expressed what he beheld in type and pledge, which was yet to reach its final culmination. The ultimate form of communication is not through the few, but when Christ shall come and abide, the Teacher and the Sanctifier, of all the truly regenerate. Joel 2: 28, predicts "the day when the spirit of God shall be poured out on all flesh." Jer. 31: 34, "And they shall teach no more every man his neighbour, and every man his brother, saying, Know the Lord: for they shall all know me, from the least of them unto the greatest of them, saith the Lord." Then shall the necessity of all prophetic instruction be superseded, and the prophetic order itself swallowed up in the indwelling of the Spirit, in each and every believer.

Different Classification Proposed.—A somewhat different classification has been proposed by some corresponding to the three leading dispensations, viz.: the Patriarchal, Mosaic and Christian. This was the classification favored by Dr. Moore, formerly of Richmond, Va., now dead, in his "Prophets of the Restoration." (See Commentary).

1. In the Patriarchal the form of divine communication was theophanic.
2. In the Mosaic, theopneustic.
3. In the Christian, theologic. In this, the will of God is made known by divine writings, the living Word. The present form is the only one that can be really universal. The prophets in this form meet us now, not in prophetic office, but in the prophetic word. The next will be the return of Christ, and the completion of the circle, back again to the theophanic, when "the pure in heart shall see God," and be admitted to His presence in heaven.

The prophetic office itself is divided into *three great eras*, corresponding to the three great dispensations to which they are referred.

1. *Theophanic.*—This extends from Moses to Samuel. In this the office was rarely filled. There was no regular succession of prophets.
2. *Theopneustic.*—From Samuel to Hosea. This is the era of the prophets of action, who were mainly occupied with the present, and so left but few writings behind them.
3. *Theologic.*—This period is marked by inspired men. It began with Hosea. The whole period of phophecy during this era looked more to future events. All the books

were written during this period, and hence it is called the Theologic era, or marked revelation of truth. They turned away from what had gone before. The office marked the mercy of God's grace to men. The last phase culminated in the incarnation of the Son of God. He assumed our human nature, and dwelling among us, became the personal Word.

II. THE PROPHETIC ORDER.

The law of Moses contemplated and made preparation for the prophets, as it did also for the kings. It is plain that, though coming from Moses, the scheme of divine communication was not to end with him, but it was to be perpetuated by others like unto him. As to the government, the people were not provided with kings immediately after Moses, but were first put under priests; subsequently were organized under judges; and, finally, the kingdom was established. So of the prophetic order, it was contemplated in the law, but did not begin at once. The term "prophet" was general at first. God at first was consulted through the priests. The prophets appeared only sporadically as it were. Finally, a continuous and permanent order was created, from Samuel onward, as kings were from Saul and David.

A "prophet," in its *wider sense*, denotes any one favored with divine communications. In Gen. 20 : 7, Abraham is called a prophet; in Ps. 105 : 15, David is referred to as a prophet: "Touch not mine anointed, and do my prophets no harm." In Acts 2 : 30, David is again called prophet.

In the *technical and more restricted sense*, the term "prophet" belongs to those not only invested with the gift of prophecy, but especially to those who were invested with the prophetic office. A distinction is made between *donum propheticum* and *munus propheticum*. In an official sense, David was not a prophet, but a king. In this sense, Moses was more than a prophet, though in Hosea 12 : 13, he is called a prophet. He was the great exemplar, the great lawgiver of Israel.

There were other prophets in the time of Moses. In Ex. 15 : 20; Num. 12 : 2, Miriam is called a prophetess. Eldad and Medad, and the seventy elders are called prophets, in Num. 11 : 25, 26. In Judges 2 : 1, probably an angel speaks, yet men of God are spoken of as his messengers, *e. g.*, 1 Sam. 2 : 27, "And there came a man of God unto Eli," etc. So in Judges 6 : 8, men of God are spoken of as prophets. The prophetic office, however, appears in its full and complete form for the first time in the time of Samuel, Acts 3 : 24. Before the time of Samuel prophecy was rare, as is seen from 1 Sam. 3 : 1. " The word of the Lord was precious in those days, there was no open vision." After the time of Samuel, though rare, the office was regularly transmitted, and-seems never to have been entirely suspended until the time of Malachi. Samuel was the first real prophet.

Seer and Prophet.—The opinion has been pressed by some that the seer possessed the gift of prophecy, but not the office, and thus was distinguished from prophets who had both the gift and the office. Some say it implies the office as well as the gift, and the Scriptures give the name prophet to every one who was a seer. This distinction holds good, according to the derivation of the words seer and prophet, but it is not sustained in the O. T. usage, *e. g.*, 1 Sam. 9 : 9. The name prophet and seer are both given. The words are used as synonymous. *Roeh*, seer, was applied to Samuel almost exclusively. The original word for prophet was *nabhi*, to boil up, to pour forth words, but the function of address was small. The people consulted them principally in regard to the future. Moses had this term applied to him, because he taught; but seer was the usual term applied to Samuel. After the change noted in 1 Sam. 9 : 9, the word prophet was revived, and became the standard. In 1 Chron. 29 : 29, we have three terms for prophet.

The Call of the Prophets.—The call of the Prophets come immediately from God himself, Amos 7 : 15, " Go, prophesy unto my people Israel." Jer. 1 : 4, " The word of the Lord came unto me; " Ezek. chaps. 1 and 2. The charge laid on Isaiah in the sixth chapter has been supposed by many to be his original call, but is more probably a re-investiture, designed to fit him for a new and special work, like that of John in Rev. 1 : 10; or Paul in Acts 22 : 17. In the call of prophets, human instrumentality is only once mentioned, and that was in the case of anointing Elisha by Elijah, in 1 Kings 19 : 16. In the 19th verse, " cast his mantle upon him." This was a symbolic act. This departure from the ordinary custom was peculiar. The prophets then had to act in the functions of the theocracy. The absence of all allusion to human agency shows that prophets probably had no rite of induction into office. In Deut. 34 : 9, Moses laid

• the head of the prophetic order

דברים – the any times.

his hands on his successor Joshua, to show the impartation of the Spirit, but there is no good reason for supposing there was any such ceremony in the line of the prophets. In Ps. 105: 15, the term "anointed" occurs parallel with the term "prophet." In Is. 61: 1, the same term is used. Anointing is symbolical of the Holy Spirit, and hence it is inferred that unction was as customary in the installation of prophets as of kings. The only case where it is spoken of or commanded, is in 1 Kings 19: 16, "And Elisha * * * shalt thou anoint to be prophet in thy room." But in this case there is no mention of its actual occurrence. When Elijah was taken up into heaven, his mantle fell upon Elisha as a symbol and pledge, that a double portion of Elijah's spirit should rest upon him, 2 Kings 2: 10. But the prophets in most cases stood in no such relation of succession as Joshua to Moses, and Elisha to Elijah. There is no propriety in any such inductions to office. The possession of the spirit of God was a sufficient induction.

Age of the Prophets.—The priests entered upon their work at a precise and regulated time. This probably was not the case with prophets, called at God's time. The only one whose age is especially mentioned, is Ezekiel, 1: 1—30 years. It is here insinuated that Ezekiel began to prophesy when thirty years old, but he was a priest, and this may account for it. Being of priestly origin, and debarred by the captivity from entering the priesthood, he was called at the same age as in the priesthood. He is the only one whose age is mentioned at the beginning. Zechariah was called when "a young man," 2: 4. Samuel when "a child." 1 Sam. 3: 1, "The child Samuel." So also Jeremiah, 1: 6. "Behold, I can not speak, for I am a child." Daniel when a child or youth, for a different term is used in the Hebrew (Dan. 1: 7.) From the great length of Hosea's ministry, 60 years, it has been inferred that he entered upon it at a very early age. Haggai, 2: 3, must have begun his prophetic work when advanced in life. He saw the temple in its glory.

In 1 Sam. 10: 5-10 we read of a "company of prophets." The "hill of God" was probably Gibeah. In 1 Sam. 19: 20, another company at Naioth in Ramah, Samuel's birthplace, is mentioned. Both Saul and his messengers were overcome, when they met the prophets, and they prophesied also. The "hill of God" may have been so called because it was the abode of these prophets, or perhaps because they were passing it. Others say there is no evidence for this. The word *Naioth* means habitations, and this was the common name for the residence of the prophets. In the Targum it is translated "schools" or "house of instruction." In 2 Kings 22: 14, we have the same term, "college," whence we obtain the expression "schools of the prophets." The Bible terms are not applicable to our idea. These schools, or company of prophets, are not heard of in Judah after the time of Samuel. In 2 Kings 22: 14, college or prophetic school is not meant, but "ward." Huldah, the prophetess, lived in the lower part or ward of the city. There is no authority for saying these companies of prophets were to be permanent. They were establishments constructed for the time and place, and they ceased with the exigency that brought them into existence. They were not schools for instruction to train men for the prophetic office, but they were bands of men, as the term implies, already invested with the office, and with a power sufficient to affect all coming into contact with them. The fact, then, would appear to be this: that they were men of God brought together, so that under the direction of Samuel they might be centers of reformation, in the midst of great apostasy.

Music.—As music was mentioned in 1 Sam. 10: 5–10, it has been argued that singing formed part of their exercises. That music was taught is plausible, and it has been conjectured that thus David may have learned to become "the sweet singer of Israel." In 1 Chron. 25: 1, David distributed the service of song among the Levites, who are spoken of as prophets.

Historians.—As the prophets were the historiographers of the nation, it has also been supposed from 1 Chron. 29: 29, that recording the history of God's people was a part of the work of the prophets.

Sons of the Prophets.—It has been supposed that "sons of the prophets" formed an analogous company in Israel. In the history of Elijah and Elisha we have frequent mention of the sons of the prophets, *e. g.*, Kings 4: 38; 6: 1. These sons of the prophets were pupils or adherents of the prophets, residing in considerable numbers at times, as would appear from the passages above cited.

Maintenance of the Prophets.—From 2 Kings 4: 38–44 we see that, though not monastic, or celibates, yet contributions were made for their maintenance. There were communities at Bethel, 2 Kings 2: 3; Jericho and Gilgal.

• who recorded in Ramah a [?] neighborhood.

• a quarter of the city.
• [?] street of [?].

[?] [?] God came together [?] [?]
[?] [?] of [?]. form a circle.

[?] = peoples or other ones of [?] [?]
together in [?]. without rows of [?]
a community of good. preached was such
by [?] [?]

Two of these places, Bethel and Gilgal, were prominent seats of idolatrous worship. Perhaps this shows reason why the prophets intended them to be centers of Reformation, and opposed to idolatry. How long these institutions continued is not known. Amos 7:14, is the only place where they are mentioned after the time of Elisha. He says "I was no prophet, neither was I a prophet's son." In 2 Kings 9:1, Elisha sent one of them to anoint Jehu. The sons of the prophets were sometimes delegated to act in the place of a prophet, as in the above passage. Some were inspired though not all of them. In 2 Kings 3:5, those at Bethel knew and told Elisha that Elijah would be taken away. It does not appear that the prophets were ordinarily taken from these institutions, or received any special training for their work. Elisha was trained by Elijah, but this was a peculiar case and a rare exception. Absence of training does not exclude providential preparation.

Mode of Life.—Of the mode of life of the prophets little is said. Only incidentally is it alluded to, so that we infer that in most respects it was like that of other men. As an appropriate dress for their work, they wore a garment of hair, *e. g.*, in Zech. 13:4, "Neither shall they wear a rough garment to deceive." Is. 20:2, "Go and loose the sackcloth from off thy loins." This perhaps is the same referred to in 2 Kings 1:8, where Elijah is called a "hairy man." This official dress was the mantle which Elijah cast upon Elisha. This was not worn as by an ascetic, but as a mourner's dress, mourning for the sins of the people, as a preacher of repentance, Dan. 9:18; Ezek. 24:18.

Their Homes.—The prophets usually dwelt in their own houses. Some of them were married, and had families—Isaiah 7:1, Samuel, Ezekiel 24:3. Jeremiah 16:2, were forbidden to marry. Some of them had servants, *e. g.*, Elijah had Elisha in constant attendance; Elisha had Gehazi; Jeremiah had Barak.

Inspiration.—As to inspiration it would seem to have been temporary, *e. g.*, Saul had only temporary inspiration, 1 Sam. 10:10. The seventy elders, in Num. 11:25, prophesied, but did not add, *i. e.*, they did not continue to prophesy. Our version conveys just the contrary, "prophesied, and did not cease." Those who were permanently in the prophetic office, seem not to have been under the permanent influence of the Spirit. What would seem to have been from foresight, they only knew when communicated, and what it was. This was the case with Moses, Lev. 24 : 12. He did not judge until the will of the Lord was made known. So in the case of Samuel, his own private thought is distinguished from that of God. This is shown in his dealings with the sons of Jesse, 1 Sam. 16 : 6, 7. God told him the right one. Nathan first told David to build the house of the Lord, but afterward told him God had forbidden it, 2 Sam. 7 : 8. All this is important in showing the nature of prophetic power. They knew and exercised, not at all times, but as God told them to speak. Elisha said, "The word of the Lord came unto them." This shows the distinction between their ordinary and inspired condition. Hence it is said by some that the spirit of prophecy is intermittent, in the way of transient impression, and not *pro modum*, John 14 : 16, 17. Some think the inspiration of O. T. prophets is thus inferior to that of the apostles. From Num 12 : 6-8, it is supposed that there are different modes of revelation. The circumstances are these : Aaron and Miriam had resisted the leadership of Moses. At this time Moses was the chief organ of divine communication. The revelations of the others are shown to be, from their inferiority of character, subordinate to his, by their intrinsic character, and by the way they were made known. There was no sufficient reason for believing this was permanent. When the prophets were raised up, "like unto Moses," why should not the Lord speak to them as to Moses? Deut. 34 : 10, refers to the age immediately succeeding Moses, and so need not be applied to the entire condition. Moses beheld the similitude of God, and spake with him face to face. If the former passages are made to cover the period of all the prophets, it does not confer on them the same power as on Moses, but shows they are thereby only inferior to Moses in the special way of receiving their communications. Moses talked with God face to face, while the others received theirs only by signs, visions, etc.

This question is principally important only as it relates to the state of mind of the prophets when they received their message. Hengstenberg maintains that the ordinary faculties of the mind—consciousness, understanding, etc.,— of the prophet were for the time suspended, and only the spiritual faculties awake :—that they were in an ecstatic state when they prophesied. It is true that this was the case sometimes; it was so in visions. So with the prophets, their minds were completely absorbed in what they were

words used. Word of the Lord came on them a

per modum impressionis transeuntis

et non habitus.

∴ in spirit of prophecy had to be inferior to

... gifts in whom the Spirit abode

permanently. —

- subsequent ... of the people.

going to say, or rather in what was within them. Dan. 8: 27, "And I, Daniel, fainted, and was sick certain days." He was physically exhausted. This also was occasionally the case with the apostles, as Peter was in a trance when he saw the sheet let down from heaven, Acts 10: 10. John also, while in Patmos. The apostle Paul was caught up into the third heaven, 2 Cor. 12: 2, 3. It cannot be argued from these that the prophets always received their impressions in this way, any more than that the apostles did. Usually they were in their ordinary state of mind. Some impressions are produced by their writings in which it is seen that all their functions were at work. This is evident from the fact that their peculiarities of style are brought out as in profane writers. This has been the belief of the church and the apostolic fathers.

Inward suggestion.—It would appear from the scanty hints on this subject that divine communications were usually by inward suggestion, and these they were able to distinguish from their ordinary thoughts in some manner which we can not understand. There were also other ways.

Audible voice.—As in 1 Sam. 3: 4, "The Lord called Samuel, and he answered, Here am I." Num. 7: 8, 9, Moses. At the baptism of Jesus, Matt. 3: 17. At the transfiguration, Matt. 17: 5. Paul's conversion, Acts 9: 4. John 12: 28, 29, "I have both glorified it, and will glorify it again."

Angels were sometimes employed to communicate to the prophets, as in Dan. 9: 21, "Even the man Gabriel, whom I had seen in vision," etc., "touched me."

Visions.—Sometimes these announcements were made known by visions. Some writers have gone to the extreme of denying that the prophets had any visions at all. They claim that this was only the form or dress in which they clothed what they wished to say. But there can be no doubt but that visions were really presented to their minds as they record them. When given in detail, it is said such minutiæ would not remain. These are more frequent in some later prophets than in others. This shows vividness. Visions were more vivid with the later prophets, *e. g.*, Ezekiel, Daniel and Zechariah; also Amos 7; Is. 6; Jer. 1. Visions were, 1. Of sensible objects, as when Ezekiel sees the temple, 8: 3; 11: 1. 2. *a.* Of symbolic objects as representative images of another order of creation. *b.* Of its sacred symbols of the sanctuary, *e. g.*, Ezekiel's vision of the cherubim of the High Priest; of the candlestick, in the vision of Zachariah, chaps. 3 and 4. *c.* Or as symbols may be natural emblems, as in Jeremiah's vision, 1: 13, of a "seething pot," *i. e.*, evils which were to come upon the people. Also Daniel's visions of the four beasts, Dan. 7. 8. Visions of supersensuous beings. God appears in visions; so do angels, Is. 6.

Sometimes the prophets sought for revelations before they were given, *e. g.*, Daniel in the case of Nebuchadnezzar's dream. In most cases, however, revelations were unsolicited. Upon one occasion, Elisha asked for a minstrel, 2 Kings 3: 15, and when the minstrel played, the hand of the Lord came upon him. Ordinarily no external aid seems to have been used. Dan. 12: 8; 2 Peter 12: 10. The prophets did not always understand the meaning of what was revealed to them. In Zech. 1: 9–19, an angel interpreted to Zechariah.

CLASSIFICATION OF THE PROPHETS.

Before entering upon the subject specifically, it may be of advantage to us to take a general survey of the classes and groups into which it is divided. It will thus prepare us for a better understanding of the whole.

Number of Prophets.—There are preserved in the O. T. the names of thirty-eight prophets, three prophetesses, and six or seven others, whose names are not given. These are but a small proportion of the whole number. The companies of prophets, the language of Scripture shows to be great companies gathered at the centre of influence. These were inspired men throughout the kingdom for mutual encouragement and teaching. In 2 Kings 2: 7–16, we read of fifty prophets, or fifty men of the sons of the prophets at Jericho. In 1 Kings 18: 4, we read of one hundred prophets being saved by pious Obadiah. He hid them in caves from the persecutions of Jezebel. There were also idolatrous prophets, *e. g.*, 1 Kings 18: 19, we find the prophets of Baal, 450; and the prophets of Astarte, 400, who ate at Jezebel's table. If so many were employed in a false religion, why not at least an equal number in the service of the true religion? We find only vague expressions during the period where more are named. 2 Chron. 24: 19; 33: 18; 36: 15. These inspired men only formed the perma-

* [illegible handwritten notes]

nent witnesses of God; they supplied the place of ordinary teachers. Only the more prominent are mentioned or referred to in the sacred records, so we infer there were not only one or two at a time, but scores and hundreds in every age, even when not named. This great body of prophets who were the depositories of God's will, have been variously classified

CLASSIFICATION.—1. The Anonymous Prophets, and those mentioned.—The anonymous were by far the greater in number and aggregate influence. All were alike in inspiration and authority. Both those whose names have been given and those whose names have not been preserved, have played an important part in sacred history, but those named were most prominent, hence their names are preserved for us in the Bible.

2. Canonical and Extra-Canonical.—The Canonical were charged with the teaching of God's people in all ages, and accordingly they have left writings which have been recorded in the sacred book. These comprise all whose names are mentioned as authors of books in the O. T., and also the authors of Joshua, Judges, 1 and 2 Samuel, and 1 and 2 Kings, which by credible tradition are classed among prophets. The Extra-Canonical prophets were no less inspired, but their commission was to their contemporaries exclusively. They either left no writings at all, or such as were to have no place in the canon, and hence, what they communicated was not intended for a permanent rule of faith. Elijah, Elisha, and others, who were Extra-Canonical, have a larger place in the books than those whose works have been preserved. This division is not the same as the former. Some that were not Canonical were of great influence, and even second to none others, *e. g.*, Elijah. Some of the anonymous prophets or writers were authors of historical books already mentioned, and preserved for us in the sacred canon.

3. The Former and Latter Prophets.—The Former prophets were authors of the six historical books already mentioned. The Latter prophets were the authors of the strictly prophetical books. These terms, Former and Latter, have reference not to the time of the composition of the books, but are due simply to the order of the books in the Hebrew canon. The Former prophets were those immediately following the Pentatauch. Judges and Samuel were written before the prophetic books, while Kings were writ-

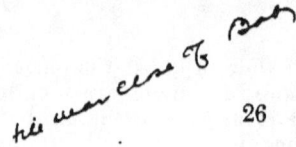

ten after. The Former prophets were all anonymous, and by unknown authors, except Joshua. None of the strictly prophetical books, so-called, are anonymous, but their names are found either in the books themselves, or attached to the close. The reason for this is that prophecy requires divine authentication attached to the person, his character and history. It was essential that the person of the prophet should be known. History is authenticated by being proved to be a true narrative. This classification does not embrace such prophetical works as are found in other parts of the canon, *e. g.*, Lamentations of Jeremiah, and certain Psalms, such as may have been written by other prophets. The book of Daniel stands in the Hebrew Bible, not among the prophetical books, but in the Hagiographa. Some say it was because the book of Daniel was written in exile, and out of the Holy Land, that it was excluded from the prophecies, but this furnishes no sufficient reason, for the same is true of Ezekiel. Others allege the reason to be that the collection of the prophets was completed before the book of Daniel was written, and hence it found its place in the later division. This is based on two false assumptions. 1. It is claimed that the book of Daniel is not genuine, not written by him, but is of a later date, and written by another hand. 2. It is assumed that different parts of the canon were collected at widely different periods of time, instead of all at once, as it really was. The true reason why Daniel is found among the Hagiographa is that Daniel was not a prophet in the strict and official sense. He was an inspired man, but did not exercise prophetic ministry among the people, as Ezekiel and Jeremiah and Isaiah did. He held a political station—prime minister at Babylon. The character of the contents of this book justifies us in classifying it among the prophets, in our present classification.

Turning our attention to the Latter prophets, we find they may be classified into the Major and Minor prophets. This has reference to the size or length, and not to the quality or rank.

A. *The Major prophets* are three: Isaiah, Jeremiah, Ezekiel; to which, for reasons already assigned, we may join Daniel, though it is not so long. Properly it belongs to an intermediate place between the two classes.

B. *The Minor prophets* are twelve in number. In all the ancient catalogues of Scripture, they are regarded as one, under the name of "the twelve," "the twelve prophets."

On account of their brevity, they were combined for convenience, and for preserving them from destruction. Though thus combined, they are entirely independent in authority. Their arrangement among themselves is, for the most part, chronological. This is denied, but it may be said—

a. There are seven out of the twelve books whose dates are known, and they stand in proper chronological order.

b. This principle determines the position and regular succession in other parts of the canon, *e. g*, in the Major prophets; but this is not the case in the Hagiographa, because they were liturgical, and other reasons make change in them.

c. Tradition favors this. Jerome says those prophetical books having no title belong to the reign of kings named in the books preceding them.

d. There is nothing in the books themselves to show that they do not stand in chronological order. The order is determined not by the time when the books were written, for then Hosea would come after Joel; nor by the absolute time of the beginning of each prophet's ministry, for then Jonah would precede the others, 2 Kings 14: 25; but the order is determined by the beginning of that portion of their ministry covered by those books which bear their names.

The arrangement of the Minor prophets among themselves, as well as their arrangement in relation to the Major prophets, differs in the Septuagint from that in the Hebrew canon. In the Septuagint, Hosea is followed by Amos, probably because both relate to the ten tribes of Israel. After them, comes Micah in the Septuagint, which relates to both Israel and Judah. In the other cases the Hebrew order is retained. It seems that the Septuagint departed from the Hebrew because of territorial reasons, boundary being followed.

The Major prophets, being the larger and more important, stand first in order in the Hebrew Bible. In the Septuagint, the order is reversed, perhaps because of chronological reasons; or perhaps the Minor prophets, because they begin with Israel and end with Judah, stand first, as the Major prophets all relate to Judah, and thus all the prophets of Judah came together. Hosea, the first of the Minor prophets, began before Isaiah, the first of the Major prophets. Or because the Major prophets all belong to

Judah, and so correspond with the end of the Minor prophets.

This division of the prophets just given, into Major and Minor, is purely external and formal. It does not affect the authority or character. There is more breadth and fulness in Micah and Zachariah, and ampler instructions as to the Messiah, than in Jeremiah.

Further divisions to be made in the prophets have more vital connection with the nature of the work, and the themes on which they respectively dwell: (1.) Divisions as to the sphere of labor, and the tribes; (2.) Periods of their ministry.

4. Division according to sphere of labor.—The sphere of the prophets' labor is divided into the prophets of Judah, and the prophets of Israel. The prophets of Israel are Hosea, Amos, Jonah; all the rest are prophets of Judah. The book of Jonah is the record of a special mission to Nineveh, but is mainly designed for the benefit of the covenant people. The distribution of the prophets between the two kingdoms into different fields of labor, has some points of analogy with the divisions of apostolic labors to the circumcision and uncircumcision. The gospel of the uncircumcision was committed to Paul, yet he wrote the Epistle to the Hebrews. Peter admitted the first Gentile convert into the church, although his mission was to the circumcision. So there was a division of labor in the O. T. times. But we must remember that the existence of distinct kingdoms was in itself schismatic and sinful. It was never recognized as lawful. The tribes of Israel were one, and formed the one chosen people of God. A writing came from Elijah, the prophet of the ten tribes, to King Jehoram of Judah, 2 Chron. 21: 12. Nahum was taken from Israel to labor in Judah. Amos from Judah to Israel. The prophets extended their reformatory work over both kingdoms. Thus it was in the period we are now discussing. Hosea and Amos occasionally addressed themselves to Judah. Isaiah and Micah sometimes have regard to Israel, although they were prophets of Judah.

5. Division by Periods.—The prophets may again be divided with reference to the periods to which they belonged, the Assyrian and Chaldean. The design of the prophets is to teach the lessons of the schism, etc., and to record the judgment (Assyrio-Babylonish judgment) of God for the good of the church. The work of judgment exhib-

· also parts 2 [strikethrough] to ask whether they are equal.

· have the other predictions respect Earlier we

a at any rate by some one under his influ

ited the forbearance of God, and gave the people time for repentance. Idolatry required a violent corrective. In the fulfillment of ancient threatenings of the law of Moses, this great empire of Asia was raised up for punishment. In the successive stages we see God's mercy in giving opportunity for repentance. The empire of Assyria was raised up, and succeeded in overthrowing the ten tribes, the stronger but more sinful of the two. This empire was not permitted to overthrow Judah, the weaker. The warning thus given to Judah was ineffectual. Having disregarded it, Babylon was erected, and they were given into its power. Judah was carried into captivity, and held therein until the time of Cyrus, when it was restored. The lessons of prophecy corresponded to the necessities of the people at the time, and reflect the spiritual wants of the people at that particular time. Prophets were raised up at each successive stage of this severe but salutary lesson. The wants of the time are determined : 1. By the condition of the people. 2. By God's purposes respecting them. These different epochs define the various prophetic periods. Of these periods, the first is :

A. *The Assyrian period*, embracing the prophets prior to, and contemporary with, the Assyrian invasion, which overthrew Israel and threatened Judah. To this period belong eight prophets, one half of the whole number. Three belong to Israel, Hosea, Amos, Jonah. Five to Judah, Joel, Obadiah, Isaiah, Micah, Nahum.

B. *The Chaldean period*, embracing the prophets prior to, or contained within, the period of the Babylonish invasion under Nebuchadnezzar, by which Judah was led captive. To this period belong three, Jeremiah, Habakkuk, Zephaniah.

C. *The Period of Exile*, during which Judah was in the land of oppressors. To this period belong Daniel and Ezekiel.

D. *The Period of Restoration*, from Cyrus to the N. T. To this period belong Haggai, Zechariah, Malachi.

(1.) I. TYPICAL MESSIANIC.   (2.) II. PROPERLY MESSIANIC.

A. IMPLICIT.		B. EXPLICIT.
a. Jonah, i. 1.		
b. Nahum, ii. J.	(A.) Periods.	(B.) Person.
		Isaiah, i.
(a.) *Negative,*	(b.) *Positive.*	Micah.
a. Obadiah, i.	a. Hosea, i. } I.	Jeremiah, iii.
b. Habakkuk, ii.	d. Amos, ii. }	Daniel, ii.
		Zachariah, iv.
	f. Joel, i.	Malachi.
	e. Zephaniah, ii. } J.	
	b. Ezekiel, iii. }	
	c. Haggai, iv. }	

6. Division into Messianic and Non-Messianic.— The prophets may still further be divided with reference to their attitude concerning the coming of Christ, and the function they were to perform in preparation for his coming. *a.* The Non-Messianic, which were only typically or indirectly Messianic. *b.* The Messianic, or directly and properly Messianic.

(1.) **The Non-Messianic** prophets did not direct their thoughts to the remote future, but confined themselves to the immediate wants of the people. They comprise nearly all who precede the period of written prophecy, *i. e.*, from Samuel to Hosea. They are restricted almost exclusively to the needs of the people and the time in which they lived. They reclaimed the people from apostasy, made disclosures, and urged the people to adhere to God, but, as a rule, say nothing of the coming Messiah. During this period we find only the most scanty predictions of Christ, 2 Sam. 7: 12–16. There were only enough of this kind to keep alive the Messianic hope of the people, and to preserve their faith from extermination. The teaching was mostly by types, sufficient for the times. It is not until the lessons of the types are adequately set forth, that the Messianic prophecy becomes prominent. Yet every promise, even of temporal good, under the old covenant, foreshadowed to them better things for the future, a greater spiritual good. The predictions of this period still have a mediate reference to the Messiah. Acts 3: 24, "Yea, and all the prophets from Samuel and those that follow after, as many as have spoken, have likewise foretold of these days," is therefore true in typical import.

(2.) **The Messianic prophets** embrace all from Hosea onward who were writers of prophecy. (Those of Canaan) not only wrote concerning the present wants of the people, but also for the needs of God's people for all time to come. In these, the doctrine of the Messiah becomes very prominent, and yet in treating this theme there is no dull, lifeless uniformity on this part of the prophets. In treating of the Messiah, the substance, character, and amount of their teaching are all different. They do not develop on all sides the doctrine of Christ, but they make their approaches to this theme from different standpoints, exhibit different aspects of it, and with different degrees of fullness. But this divergence shows no discrepancy. It is possible to gather the whole up into a higher unity. They are not only har-

not by morphemes.

the material a type of the [surface], [stamp?]
of the [lemma?]. —

monious, but they are mutually self-supporting, and are supplementary to each other. Whether such a combination was possible before Christ appeared, or was fully understood, is difficult to say. However, it is plain that all these divine representations do find their counterpart in the Lord Jesus Christ. In Christ all the enigmas of prophecy are solved, and we see the consistency of what the prophets wrote concerning him.

Division according to Implicit or Explicit Disclosure concerning Christ.—These sixteen prophetical books may be further classified in respect to their manner of disclosure concerning Christ. This manner may be divided and the prophets viewed as Implicitly Messianic, and Explicitly Messianic. *a.* Implicitly Messianic furnished a link between the prophets of this and the former period. They do not in express terms speak of that which is strictly Messianic, yet their predictions obviously stand in closer connection with the Messianic prophets than the unwritten types do. *b.* The Explicitly Messianic make Christ the direct theme of prophecy. **A.** Of the **Implicitly Messianic** or transition prophets, there are only two, Jonah and Nahum. They were not contemporaries, yet they belonged to the Assyrian period, Jonah in Israel, and Nahum in Judah. The theme of both was the purpose of God with respect to Nineveh, the capital of Assyria, the prominent foe of God's people. These two prophets make entirely diverse revelations concerning the fate of Nineveh, the common foe of both nations. They appear at different times, and present Messianic lessons, from different sides.

a. Jonah, the sphere of whose work lay mainly in the ten tribes, in the time of prosperity under Jeroboam, was sent to prophesy in Nineveh, the capital city of Assryia, Jonah 4: 11. This city was selected rather than some other, because it was then the great hostile power which threatened Israel. Jonah's prophecy had a good effect. By hearkening to his message the city was spared. The contrast is, that Israel is obstinate, and hastening on to destruction, while Nineveh, the heathen enemy, is saved, Jon. 4: 11. Jonah had preached a long time to Israel, and they did not repent. He went and preached in Nineveh, and it repented at once, and was saved. The great typical lesson is that the gospel shall one day be preached to the Gentiles, and they should hear it, while God's ancient covenant people should be cast off. The great foe of Israel was spared to be its overthrow. But the time had not yet come for an actual change. God's purposes were not yet ripe. Therefore Assyria was not then substituted for Israel. Assyria still continued heathen, and Israel the favored people of God. The Gentiles should not only hear the gospel, but obey it, while Israel should be cast off, and deprived of the religion of their fathers. It was typical of what should transpire when Christ came.

b. The message of *Nahum* was for Judah, which was not to be overthrown by Assyria as Israel was. Nahum, therefore, predicts the preservation of the people of God. It is not the development of a Messianic prophecy, but this may be inferred. This disastrous overthrow of Assyria stands as a type of the overthrow of all God's enemies, the safety of God's people, and the judgments against an ungodly world. These are totally different, and yet the same. If we put them into contrast, according to Jonah, Israel is cut off; while according to Nahum Israel is saved, and the heathen cut off.

B. The rest of the prophetic books are **Explicitly Messianic**,—they teach of Christ in express terms. Here, again, we find a great variety of aspects, far greater than before. As to the character of the Messianic period, we may view it as comprising two classes. (*a.*) Those which treat of the Messianic period itself. (*b.*) Those which, in addition to that, speak of the Messiah's person. The one exhibits a negative view of the Messianic period in the light of deliverance from present and future evils; the other develops the positive character. The former declare what the Messianic period is not. The latter what it is. A future which stood in no sort of relation to the present, could not be understood by the people, but if so related that the lesson may become comparatively easy, then we must make the present the point of departure. It is thus we obtain our knowledge of spiritual things—by our own consciousness, negative and positive. Thus we get an idea of God from a knowledge of ourselves: first by denying to Him all the imperfections which we find in ourselves; second, by ascribing to Him all the perfections of what is good. So the prophets do. Some deny to that glorious period the evils of the present. Others positively prophesy blessings and benefits on that time.

(**A.**) **Messianic Periods.** Negative and Positive. (**a.**)/ *In the negative,* Obadiah belongs to the Assyrian period;

Moses. lesson = security of God's people —
find without of their enemies

we will try to calculate & show of them the
rw.
a = Equ proplem.   a. = 2
                   b. = 6

not only Eocene but Miocene

Habakkuk to the Chaldean. Both belonged to Judah. Both direct their prophecy to different yet related themes.

a. Obadiah belonged to the earlier portion of prophecy, and selected Edom, a small neighboring state, as the representative of the enemies of God. The burden of O. is the downfall of Edom. He reaches into Messianic times, and predicts that every enemy of God shall find its downfall. The book ends with the declaration, ": The Kingdom shall be the Lord's." This offers another opportunity for inculcating the same lesson in a more impressive form, which occurred in the Chaldean period, *i. e.*, the universality of His kingdom.

b. Habakkuk in the Chaldean period. A far more formidable foe than Edom had arisen. The great empire of Babylon was terrible. It gave a conception of the possible combination which might be arrayed against the people of God. It presents a spectacle of universal empire, ruling almost the whole world. It was given to Habakkuk to predict the overthrow of this huge empire, and deduce from it the same lesson Obadiah had done, the universality of God's kingdom as opposed to all others. Hab. 2 : 14, "For the earth shall be filled with the knowledge of the glory of the Lord, as the waters cover the sea." This truth could insure the downfall of Babylon, though now at the height of its power.

b. The remaining six prophets are *positively Messianic*, not only as speaking of this period as one of deliverance, but in a positive sense. They are Joel, Zephaniah, Ezekiel, Haggai, of Judah; Hosea and Amos, of Israel. They delineate in positive aspect the actual benefits of the Messianic period, yet here also is there variety in the mode of presentation.

a. Hosea takes no note of anything but the fortunes of God's covenant people, and of the Gentile nations merely as executioners of what comes upon God's people, without any reference to what shall become of them themselves. He was sent to prophesy to the ten tribes shortly before they were to be overthrown by Assyria. He was to assure the despondent pious of the glorious future awaiting God's people. The Messianic teaching in Hosea has four points: 1. The favor of God shall be restored forever. 2. The unity of the people of God under one head. No such disastrous schism as at present exists shall divide the nation. 3. Immense multiplicity of the people of God. 4. Their return.

They shall be regathered out of the dispersion, ~~so threatening~~, and be brought back to the Lord's land.

b. Ezekiel, sent to Judah when in exile, develops still more fully and minutely the blessings which the people would enjoy. He adopts the symbols of the old economy, and pushes them to greater length than Hosea did. Ezekiel describes in addition to the return, and in minute detail, the fresh partition of lands among the people, the rebuilding and measurements of the temple, and restoration of the Levitical ceremonials. This is only in a symbolic and emblematic sense. The theocracy, which seemed to be in ruins, was to be restored after the same general pattern as before, but on a much larger scale. He refers also to the destiny awaiting their heathen foes, now exulting over Israel's downfall and Judah's captivity. He declares they shall fall before the people of God. There is no mention that the Gentiles shall be partakers of the blessings of God's people.

c. Haggai comes after the exile and stands on substantially the same platform as Ezekiel, although he seems to be partially paving the way for the extension of the good news of the kingdom to the Gentiles. The government of Judah shall be protected. Whatever may perish, God's people shall be saved. The result is stated in Haggai 2: 7, "And I will shake all nations, and the desire of all nations shall come: and I will fill this house with glory, saith the Lord of hosts." The "desire of all nations" is not a personal designation of the Messiah, as satisfying the longings of mankind. It does not mean Messiah, as many have explained it. This view is true from various considerations, being supported from the prophet's own understanding of the passage. According to grammatical principles the "desire" of all nations is a collective, feminine singular. The temple seemed poor in comparison with Solomon's, which preceded it, but all the treasures of the nations shall be brought to adorn and beautify the Lord's house. Haggai does not say persons of the Gentiles should be brought into the kingdom of God, but their noblest possessions. He does not say whether they are to be voluntarily brought, or wrested from their unwilling hands. This is not explicitly declared, yet all suspense and doubt are removed by the three remaining ones, who each unambiguously affirm that the Gentiles shall share in the blessings of the Messiah's kingdom. This is set forth by each in different aspects.

- a mystery of God with [us?].
- ~~most~~ glorious form.
- a this has no prominence among his [life?]

- and the Conversion / reputation of matter

Seven = character

- should be brought + carry + created to God
  him then

d. Amos speaks of the incorporation of the Gentiles into the kingdom of God, as the result of their spiritual subjugation by Israel, 9: 12, "That they may possess the remnant of Edom, and of all the heathen, which are called by my name, saith the Lord that doeth this." That the Gentiles, like Israel, were to be called by the "Lord's name," implies that they are to come into the same relation with God as His people. This is the result of conquest by Israel. Active propagation of the gospel proceeding from the heart of the Christian church. So David must be built up as of old. There must be a Spiritual people. The Christian church must be built up and owe its existence to the Jewish church. This was in part the case. The founders of the Christian church were Jews.

e. Zephaniah, on the other hand, declares the Gentiles, like Israel, are to be purified by divine judgments, Zeph. 2: 11; 3: 8, 9. According to Zephaniah, God's providential judgments are to be the agents in bringing about the blessing.

f. Joel 2: 28, makes no mention of any active extension or propagation of God's kingdom by those included in it, nor of the effect of God's providences in breaking down obstacles, but he refers it solely to the outpouring of the Spirit of God, this being the only agency employed in the work. This is in accordance with His great promise, "I will pour out my spirit upon all flesh."

(B) Person of the Messiah.—The last class of Messianic prophets are those who make revelations, not only concerning the character of the Messianic period, but also concerning the person of the Messiah. This class embraces the six remaining prophets, all of whom belong to Judah. The Personal prophets are Isaiah, Micah, Jeremiah, Daniel, Zechariah, and Malachi. There is a double reason for confining these explicit disclosures concerning Messiah's person to Judah. First, because the kingdom of the ten tribes was not to survive, as the kingdom of Judah should, till the advent of the Messiah. It was destroyed by Assyria, and never be revived again. It was to be superfluous, therefore, to supply them with marks of the coming Messiah. Second, the great body of the truly pious, and that in which the proper succession of the covenant people lay, was in Judah. They greatly outnumber the prophecies of Israel, and the disclosures made to Judah far surpass those made to Israel. So, also, Messianic disclosures were limited.

These six prophets, who make distinct mention of the person of the Messiah, are distributed through all four of the prophetic periods. There are two in the Assyrian period; two in the period of Restoration; and one each in the Chaldean and Exile periods. Isaiah and Micah belong to the Assyrian; Jeremiah, Chaldean; Daniel, Exile; Zechariah and Malachi, Restoration.

a. Jeremiah makes the most scanty revelation of the person of the Messiah. His period was the downfall of Judah. He predicts the Messiah as the righteous king, in contrast with the degenerate monarch of his own day. He is to restore, not only his people, but all things to his will.

b. Micah adds the Messiah shall be not only a virtuous king of David's ancient race, but a divine monarch, and an effectual defense and protection against all foes, however powerful.

c. Daniel contrasts Christ's kingdom with the utmost potency with the greatest kingdoms of the world. He thus carries the teachings of the Messiah to the greatest extent. In symbol, he represents the kingdoms of the world as brutal, figured by beasts of uncommon kinds; on the other hand, he represents the Messiah as the Son of Man, 7: 13.

d. Isaiah adds to what has thus far been set forth, his prophetic office as teacher of the nations, and the fact of his vicarious sacrifice for sin is set forth most clearly by this prince of the prophets.

e. Zechariah combines with his kingly office that of his priestly office, making him a priest upon his throne, as well as the Good Shepherd disowned by his flock, thus representing the sufferings he should endure as a priest.

f. Malachi predicts the Messiah as a judge, refining and purifying by the fires of his justice, separating the righteous from the wicked.

All of these prophets except Jeremiah present special marks of identification, marks by which he may be known when he comes. Isaiah foretells his birth from a virgin mother, and his ministry in Galilee. Micah foretells his birth in Bethlehem. Daniel mentions the time of his appearing. It should be at the expiration of the seventy weeks. Zechariah speaks of his riding into Jerusalem upon an ass. Malachi, his being preceded by a forerunner, or one who should "come in the spirit and power of Elias," as we read it elsewhere.

an in its change

[Various passages quoted or used in support of our present "Division of Prophets." From the Minor prophets: Hosea 1:10, 11; 3:5. Joel 2:28-32. Amos 9:11-15. Obadiah 1:31. Micah 4:1-3; 5:2. Hab. 2:14. Zeph. 2:11; 3:8, 9. Hag. 2:6, 7. Zech. 6:12, 13; 9:9; 13:17. Mal. 3:1-3; 4:5. From the Major prophets: Is. 7:14-16; 9:1-7; 53:1-12. Jer. 33:15-17. Ezek. chs. 38, 39, 40-48. Dan. 2:44-45; 9:24-27.]

ASSYRIAN PERIOD.

I.—PROPHETS OF THE KINGDOM OF ISRAEL.

They should not be taken at random, for there is order here. They must not be massed together, nor isolated, so that the connection may be lost. They were part of the divine scheme, a system of training to which the Israelites were subjected, and were conceived in order. The ministry of each particular prophet fills its approprite place in the era to which he belongs. The complete study of the prophets embraces:

1. Each book in its own individual character, and absolute amount of prophecy which it contains.

2. In its relation to its own group or period. The functions which belong to it individually and how all work together.

3. Relation of the mission of each period to the grand system of prophetic teaching which embraces all the prophets.

4. Relation of the work of preparation considered as a whole to the entire scheme of training to which Israel was subjected under the whole O. T., for this preparation by the medium of the prophets is only a part in a greater whole. *a.* Legal preparation by Laws of Moses. *b.* Providential preparation by the history of the people in the historical books—negative and positive. *c.* Individual preparation: the subjective preparation in the poetical books, the religious experiences of inspired and sanctified men, their inward and outward trials which have their bearing upon the Son of Man.

We begin with the consideration of the prophets of Israel, because:

(1.) This is probably the chonological order. Although the prophets of Israel are in general synchronous with the first periods of Judah, yet Hosea, the first prophet of Israel, began before Joel, the first prophet of Judah.

(2.) It enables us to complete the prophets of one kingdom before beginning the others.

(3.) The future disclosures made to Israel, as well as the revelations concerning the Messiah, are less full and clear than those granted to the prophets of Judah, and thus there is progress. In order to understand the whole character of their ministries we must look at **the providential circumstances which determined their character.**

I. *Intrinsic character of the kingdom and the domestic and foreign relations of Israel.*

a. It was inherently sinful in character, being founded on schism and apostasy, leaving the true worship of God in Jerusalem for the worship of false gods in Bethel and Dan. The very existence of this kingdom was a crime against God. The perpetuity of the kingdom involves this twofold guilt.

b. There was universal corruption. (1) The kings universally were wicked from a scriptural point of view. In Judah some were good. (2) The abandonment, by the people, of the true worship of God, followed by awful sins and violence, which are rebuked by the prophets, in both princes and people. One of the fruits of this is to be found in the fact that there were was no regular hereditary succession to the throne, but many usurpations and regicides and interregnums. Four out of seven kings during the ministry of this period were murdered, and only two transmitted the crown to their descendants, and this for one generation. There were repeated civil wars, and two periods of anarchy, during which no monarch sat upon the throne for several years. (This seems a necessary inference from the history, though not expressly stated) The ten tribes having thus cut themselves off from the people of God and his divinely appointed worship, and having become more opposite to the character of God's chosen people, the question arises, How will God treat them and deal with them? The book of Chronicles omits the history of the ten tribes altogether, as not belonging to the theocratic history of the kingdom of God at all, and confines itself to Judah.

during this period

God's purpose with respect to them

abolition of worship of Baal.

The actual influence of queens & of
prophets in Judah.

II. *Purpose of God respecting it.*

a. His forbearance hitherto is shown by preserving it for nearly two hundred years in a moderate state of peace and prosperity. The schism began with the revolt of Jeroboam I, B. C. 975; death of Jeroboam II., B. C. 784; shortly before which the latter period begins with the period of the prophecy of Hosea.

b. God's favor is shown by interrupting the course of degradation from Jeroboam to Ahab, by: (1) Ministries of Elijah and Elisha. (2) After Ahab by placing on the throne the princes of Jehu. Jehu was made king, 884 B. C. The first century of the schism, or, more exactly, the first 90 years from the original revolt of Jeroboam to the fall of the house of Ahab, was one of growing corruption, until Ahab and his heathen wife renounced the worship of God entirely for the heathen gods. This process of degradation was broken off by placing Jehu on the throne. The preparation for this was made by the period of Elijah and Elisha, whose ministry extended to Joash, the grandson of Jehu, and under Jehu there was a zealous reform, for which he was commended by God. Although the golden calves were still retained, Jehu was of marked ability, and the princes remained for four reigns, upward of a century, as God had promised to Jehu, 2 Kings 10: 30. Under the reign of these princes there was prosperity to Israel, and deliverance from their foreign oppressors, and victory over them. Under Jeroboam II. there was an extension of the kingdom to the limits reached by Solomon, 2 Kings 14: 25.

c. The raising up of prophets to labor among them for their admonition and salvation, and to show that they were not yet to be cast off, combined ministries of Hosea, Amos, Jonah, besides others, as Oded, 2 Chron. 28: 9, and many more. All these measures failed to effect any thorough reform of the people of God at large, and the period of forbearance was drawing to a close, and was to be followed by one of judgment. The term of the house of Jehu was nearly at an end; his third descendant, Jeroboam II., had nearly reached the end of his reign. His successor, Zachariah, was to reign only six months. The great Assyrian power (B. C. 721) was to overthrow Israel, capture Samaria, and take the people into captivity.

Nature of their Ministry.—The character of the people and the designs of God respecting them are the main elements that determine their necessities and show the nature of the ministry. This ministry was not to be exercised by a single individual. Even as our Lord sent out his disciples two by two, both for mutual aid and countenance, as well as that in the mouths of two or three witnesses his word should be established, so here the prophets were to supplement each other, to seize the truth on different sides, to teach distinct though related lessons. In regard to Hosea, Amos, and Jonah, there was not the full amount of instruction in any one of them, but in the combination of the lessons which they severally teach and in regarding them altogether as one united ministry. Yet we must not lose sight of their individual peculiarities. We must show their close connection, and how each had its own distinctive mission to fulfil, but all harmonize and cooperate in the accomplishment of the common end. It is apparent that a people so given to sin, and in the prospect of judgment, needed:

1. *A ministry of rebuke and denunciation.* This is a characteristic of these three prophets, and is in marked contrast with the (three) prophets of Judah. This denunciation and rebuke is administered by Hosea directly, Jonah indirectly, Amos in both ways. Hosea and Amos performed their direct work by threatening in so many terms the complete destruction of the kingdom, and foretelling the captivity and rejection of the mass of the people, and this occupies the bulk of these books, only a few verses containing a promise of mercy. Amos threatens the overthrow of many nations around Israel who are less guilty than Israel, while as to the great power, Assyria, which was around Israel, he says not a word, leaving it to be inferred that it is to finish the mission of destroying Israel. Jonah also shows indirect proof of the same fact. The Ninevites are less obdurate than Israel, and the actual destruction of Nineveh is postponed. Yet the promises of God are not to be frustrated, mercy was in store for them and for the world, for which the judgment was to be a means to an end. No promises whatever of the proximate future are given to Israel, nothing to break the full force of the impending judgment, so that this judgment might be averted. For the present all is dark, but there is a brighter prospect beyond, after the work of judgment shall be accomplished.

2. With an entire absence of all promises for the present, they nevertheless *point forward to Messianic blessings.*

by this means to provoke them.

ominous silence

Nothing is said about the person of the Messiah, but only about the Messianic period, which is different from the contemporaneous prophets of Judah, *e. g.*, Isaiah and Micah. There the person of Messiah is treated of (*a*) in a more obscure form, sufficient for present purpose to comfort them; (*b*) not the same necessity to give marks to a kingdom which was to end long before the advent of the Messiah. For similar reasons, the Messianic period is not largely and fully dwelt upon by these prophets of Israel. They make a contrast between the evils of the present, and the glories of the future.

1. The attitudes and revelations of the prophets are different. Hosea and Amos are explicit, use express terms, Jonah implicit, by actions which foreshadow the future.

2. There is a difference in the *extent* of the revelations themselves respecting the Messianic period. Hosea tells only of the blessings to Israel, Jonah of the calling of the Gentiles, and Amos speaks of both. He unites with Hosea in announcing that the destruction of the kingdom is a necessary antecedent to the fulfilment of their hopes. That they shall be returned to God by these, and be reunited to Judah, and then the blessing shall come. Amos, with Jonah, tells of the future calling of the Gentiles, but in a different way, and different aspect. Amos foretells the spiritual subjugation of the heathen, by a power from Israel. Jonah treats of the preaching of the Gospel to all nations, and embraced by them voluntarily, while Israel remains impenitent and unbelieving. The calling of the Gentiles is implicitly connected by Jonah with the rejection of the Jews. From the N. T. we see that both were fulfiled.

3. *Personal Relations.* — Knowledge on this matter is scanty. The only thing mentioned of Hosea is the name of his father. The residence and occupation of Amos is given. The residence and father of Jonah.

4. *Citizenship.* — Hosea and Jonah belong to the Kingdom of Israel. Amos lived in Judah, but ministered to Israel. It is not stated concerning Hosea, but is inferred from knowledge concerning the others.

5. *Scene of their Ministry.* — Hosea in the ten tribes: no particular place mentioned. Amos in Bethel, 7 : 13. Jonah in Nineveh.

6. *Their writings.* — Hosea a résumé or abstract of a long ministry. Jonah and Amos record a single brief mission which in the case of Amos was a mission from Israel to

Judah. It may have been the whole of his prophetic career, but in the case of Jonah it was not, 2 Kings 14: 25.

Messianic teaching.—The prophets of Israel do not advance much on the promises made to David, but they are reiterated and re-enforced, expanded in the case of Judah.

7. *Theme.*—Hosea exclusively treats of the duty and destiny of the covenant people. Amos relates both to the covenant people and Gentile nations; Jonah exclusively to a particular Gentile nation.

8. *Form of the Prophecies.*—Hosea and Jonah symbolic actions; Amos symbolic visions.

9. All are recognized and referred to in the N. T. Hosea in Rom. 9: 25: 1 Pet. 2: 10. Amos, James in Acts 15: 16. Jonah by our Lord, Matt. 12: 39-41.

HOSEA. B. C. 784–724.

PERSON AND BOOK.

Name means salvation; from which we may perhaps infer that he was from pious parents. It is the original name of Joshua, Num. 13: 8, 16. Also, the name of the last king of Israel, 2 Kings 15: 30. He was the son of Beeri, the mention of whom does not prove him to have been a person of distinction, nor a prophet, according to the Rabbins, who say that whenever the name of the father of the prophet is given, the father also was a prophet. It is simply the oriental mode of supplying the lack of family names; called so to distinguish him from others of the same name.

It is probable that, like most of the other prophets, he was a native of Israel. (*a.*) If not we should expect it to be expressly mentioned, as in the case of Amos. (*b.*) The places mentioned in Hosea belong to the ten tribes, and the events belong to the history of the ten tribes. (*c.*) Especially (7: 5) "our king," and such expressions as " the land " (1: 2) " I have seen " (6: 10). These indicate a knowledge of the land.

Some have urged that there are unusual forms in the book which betray the northern idiom, but not enough is known of the Hebrew dialects to warrant such a statement.

Some have objected to the view of the prophet's belonging to the ten tribes; that the title of the book indicates that

by vars in meaning a distinction in all the papers the same in Hrs.

All the places mentioned are in Ds.
Events belong to hist of Ds.
6:10 implies his personal presence in Ds.

as Aquinas wrote: no one but God, an author of the moral law, might command it.

he was of Judah, because he names the kings of Judah, in whose reigns he prophesied. The kings of Judah are mentioned in full, while of the kings of Israel, only Jeroboam is mentioned. The explanation of this is not that he lived in Judah, but that he did not recognize the right of the schism of Israel, and that the king of the house of Judah was the only lawful king. This is shown by other passages, 8: 4, "They have set up kings, but not by me;" and in 3: 5, they are to come back under the rule of Judah. To these kings of Judah, he adds the name of Jeroboam, king of Israel, for a double reason. (a.) To indicate more exactly the beginning of his ministry. Uzziah's reign lasted until 26 years after the death of Jeroboam, but it was in that part of Uzziah's reign when Jeroboam was still living, that he began his ministry. (b.) Because God by His providence gave a certain kind of sanction to Jeroboam as one of the princes of Jehu, *vide* 2 Kings 14: 25-27, "He saved them by Jeroboam the son of Joash."

Ewald has a kind of intermediate theory, viz.: that the prophet at first belonged to Israel, but on account of opposition, he removed to Judah. This is only imaginative.

Marriage.—As to the account of the prophet's marriage, from ancient times interpreters have been divided. Was his faithless wife an allegory or a fact? In either case it was certainly symbolical of the Lord's relation to His erring people. It is improbable that it was a literal occurrence, for

1. God would not have commanded a holy prophet to form such a connection. (Hengstenberg) though it is not a command to form a sinful connection, as some have maintained, yet it was certainly a revolting one, would subject him to an endless amount of scandal, and thus destroy his influence.

2. The law of Moses (Lev. 21: 7) forbade a priest to marry an unchaste woman. In regard to this, the law of ceremonial purity relative to the priesthood is not to be applied to the prophet, for the priest would not even marry a divorced woman. The high priest (Lev. 21: 13, 14) could not marry a widow. But the prophets were nevertheless a sacred order of men as well as the priests, and God would not specially direct them to form alliances of this kind. Some think God could command this for he could change the moral law.

3. An argument from the third chapter in which the prophet is again required to form another such connection,

without any intimation that the former wife is dead or put away. Is this a direction to renew his connection with the woman? Or is it a direction to marry irrespective of the command? The force of this argument depends upon the interpretation to be put upon this latter command, (Chap. 3). If it is interpreted as a mere repetition of the former command, the argument has no force. If it is a new command, the argument will apply. The whole appearance of the second command is against a previous actual marriage.

4. Significant names of the children of this woman seem to show that it was merely allegorical.

5. The action of the first chapter would require years for its performance, requiring not only his marriage, but the birth of several children.

The symbolic lesson would be lost entirely, and the people would think of the scandal. The marriage is simply an allegory. [W. H. G.]

Other interpretations.—(1) To modify the meaning from literal sense to that of unchaste nature, but it is too personal. (2) A reformed harlot. But there is no mention of children born of her before marriage with Hosea. Moreover the symbolism would not be applicable to Israel. (3) Others hold to the literal interpretation and say that as Abram obeyed God in offering up Isaac, so Hosea in marrying. If God could suffer the transgression of Israel, Hosea could suffer his foul wife. But it is probably an allegory told as a parable. (4) Ewald (followed by Robinson Smith) supposes Hosea really had this experience, but without knowing at the time its significance. God prepared him in this way for deeper understanding of his prophetic work. This view relieves the difficulty, but is not consistent with the words of the prophecy. Hos. 1: 2. Jer. 2: 8 does not show that the word of the Lord was revealed in an ex post facto manner. Ewald's theory moreover, does not explain the 2nd marriage of Ch. 3.

Date.—"The word of the Lord that came unto Hosea, the son of Beeri, in the days of Uzziah, Jotham, Ahaz, and Hezekiah, kings of Judah, and in the days of Jeroboam, the son of Joash, king of Israel," Hosea 1: 1

Duration of Ministry.—Hosea 1: 1, Uzziah reigned 52 years, Jotham 16, Ahaz 16, Hezekiah 29, in all 113. It can not be supposed that Hosea was prophet during the entire reigns of all these. Jeroboam II, died 784 B. C. Uzziah survived him 26 or 27 years. From the death of Jeroboam

of such an unfortunate case.

Ewald & Smith would rather [say] the meaning but that prophet was ignorant, God purposing him to understand the [will] of God's people but not consistent with Isaiah an [Hos 1:2   cp Jer 32:8] but when that it now. guidance takes place [in] prophesying word of Lord

the name, etc.

1 Similarity to title of [illegible]
∴ not properly transferred

2 Reminiscent with [illegible]
Their off. showed inefficiency of their ~~[illegible]~~ cities

to the accession of Hezekiah, was 58 years. Supposing Hosea was prophet one year under Jeroboam, and one year under Hezekiah, his ministry would have been sixty years in length. We are not informed whether Hosea lived to see the overthrow of Samaria or not. If so, his ministry would be 65 years. If he began his ministry when 20, he was 85, when he died, the oldest of all the prophets. The truth of the title has been impugned. In answer to the charge that these statements are false, we answer:

1. Those who make them are not agreed among themselves as to the length of his ministry. Some say 55, others 40, others 30, others 20, and others still less. This disagreement betrays the insufficiency of the data.

2. The method pursued by them is inadmissible. They assume the ministry of the prophet terminated immediately after the latest event recorded in the prophecy, and that the absence of allusion to any important event shows that it did not occur during his ministry; but Hosea was not intending to give a history of all events. Ewald says he makes no mention of the invasion by the king of Assyria, and therefore it can not have transpired during his ministry, or he surely would have alluded to it. Simpson finds an allusion to the assassination of Menahem's son, Pekahiah, by Pekah, son of Remaliah.

3. The title is directly established by the statements of the book itself. In 1:4, the fall of the house of Jehu is predicted as still future. With the exception of six months Jeroboam was the last king, hence Hosea's ministry must have begun in the reign of Jeroboam. In 10:14, "as Shalman spoiled Betharbel in the day of battle." Betharbel is Arbela, a fortified town in Galilee; Shalman is Shalmaneser, whose invasion was under Hoshea, the last king of Israel, which brings us almost to the reign of Hezekiah. From the former passage he must have begun in the reign of Jeroboam; from the latter passage he must have continued to Hezekiah.

4. Diversity of length and form of titles corroborate the truth of the book. Books of Kings seem to be confirmed and the length of each reign given. Time of reigns of Judah 160 and of Israel 144 years. This obtained by saying there were times of anarchy, e. g., 2 Kings 14:21—between Jeroboam and Zachariah. Assyrian chronology dissuades from idea of interregnum between Kings. Some have been fond of giving political effects and eclipses to get chronology and

a good one agreeing with biblical record can be made out. Monuments also give testimony, some years off the record. Actually the reign of succession begins before the father's ends.

Structure of the Book—Critics are divided From the brevity of the book it is not probable that it contains all the prophcies Hosea ever uttered. Does not contain distinct discourses which we can state particularly, and their date be ascertained. Dr. Wells says there are five discourses in chronological order. German critics go to the most unwarrantable extremes, multiplying these divisions, saying that the book is compiled without any order at all. Maurer says 13 discourses; others say 29; some 17, 14, etc. and others many more. Each paragraph is searched to find an historical statement as a theme of discourse. The book is not a congeries of fragments, but is one continuous composition prepared by him near the close of his ministry, and having in condensed form the discourses of his ministry. He simply places upon record what is of permanent value to the people of God in such a form as would suit best his immediate purposes.

Ewald proposes an ingenious but artificial division. He says there are two parts corresponding to the two allegories in chaps. 1 and 2. 1–2 are the first part of the allegory and the comments: the remainder, 3–14, is the second part of the allegory and comments. This last comment has three parts: 1, Charge of sin against the people, and against particular classes; 2, Denunciation of punishment; 3, Two retrospects of ancient and better days.

Perhaps the most satisfactory division is based upon the literary form of the book. The first three chapters are emblematic. The second part of the book, from 4th to 14th chapter, is literal. Agreeably to a hint furnished by chap. 1 : 2, the former may be considered as the earlier part of the prophet's ministry. This corresponds to the contents of the text. In this the people are charged with outward sins. From the 4th chapter the tone of the book manifestly changes, and the latter division reflects the turbulent period, regicides, etc. Reason in the first three chapters for the overthrow of the kingdom clearly foretold, and announcing who shall be the authors of that judgment. In the first part of the book, the Assyrians are not mentioned by name, but in the subsequent chapters they are named. In each of these three main sections of the book are three Messianic

120 = 45 yrs less than Zr. Bib chron.
No satisfactory curve as yet. I have
no actual chron. in Bible.
  ep act by Dr. Davis. P.R. Review.

a logic in oil on plan of a sermon
by ?
Campaign Meeting at ? Evangelical

• Symbolic marriage or the prostitute
  described —
Israel worship ? God. yes great reign
of Jeroboam

passages, making the ends of as many subdivisions. Those in the first section occur at the close of each of the first three chapters. In the second section are three promissory passages, 6: 1-3; 11: 8-11; 14: 1-9. The passages are not only of increasing length, but are of growing fullness and power. They are climactic in thought. Predictions of the book relate partly to the near and partly to the remote future.

PREDICTIONS OF HOSEA.

I. Nearer predictions: (*a*) ch. 1: 4, overthrow of the house of Jehu, *cf.* 2 Kings 10: 30; 15: 10, 12. (*b*) The complete destruction of the kingdom of the ten tribes, the exile of the people, and the desolations of the land, 1: 4-6; 2: 11-13; 3: 4, *et passim*. This is burden of the book.

Locality of the Exile.—Forms of statement vary, and appear to conflict. 8: 13, "They shall return to Egypt." 9: 6, "Egypt shall gather them up, Memphis shall bury them." But, on the other hand, 11: 5, "He shall not return into the land of Egypt, but the Assyrian shall be his king, because they refused to return." 9: 3, "They shall not dwell in the Lord's land; but Ephraim shall return to Egypt and they shall eat unclean things in Assyria." 11: 11, "They shall tremble as a bird out of Egypt, and as a dove out of the land of Assyria." These varying declarations seem to be: (*a*) They shall be carried into Egypt; (*b*) not in Egypt, but Assyria; (*c*) both into Egypt and Assyria. Skeptics say this shows vacillation in mind of prophet. But (1) they hold this book to be a continuous history. But it is singular that the prophet should record these vacillations in a continuous history. Vacillations would seem to prove the book a compilation of fragments. (2) There is, however, no contradiction here. It is not necessary to suppose that the prophet was of different mind in different periods of his ministry. The meaning either is, (*a*) That while a portion of the people shall be scattered into Egypt, and find graves there, the bulk of them shall not go there, but to Assyria. (*b*) Egypt is here introduced in a symbolic sense as the land in which their fathers had been in bondage, and they should be carried not into literal Egypt, but to a land which shall be to themselves what Egypt had been to their fathers.

In 1: 7, he predicts that Judah shall not fall as Israel, but shall be miraculously delivered. *Cf.* 2 Kings 19: 35, host of Sennacherib smitten by an angel. 8: 14, subsequent destruction of Judah's cities is directly threatened. The captivity is not predicted, but presupposed, 1: 11, and 2 Kings 25: 8, 9. The destruction of the palaces of Judah by fire was fulfilled 130 years after his death, in 588, B. C.

II. Four Blessings.—In addition to these predictions, H. predicts four blessings belonging to the remote future. (*a*) 1: 10, Immense multiplication of Israel, as the sand of the sea. (*b*) Return to God and enjoyment of his favor, 2: 20, 21. (*c*) Union with Judah under King David, the lawful prince of David's line, 1: 11; 3: 5. (*d*) Their return thus united from the land of their captivity, 1: 11; 11: 11.

Each of these is disclosed in contrast with existing or threatening evils. These evils are: (*a*) The impending destruction of the kingdom; (*b*) Their apostasy from God; (*c*) Their schism from Judah; (*d*) Threatened captivity. From the judgments upon Israel, they might fear they would be extirpated, and what is to become of the promises? H. discloses that the promises shall abide in their full force. The work of purgation shall be the means of fulfilling the promise. The schism between Israel and Judah shall terminate. **III. Period of great success.**—Earlier chapters of Israel well supplied. 2: 5-12; 2: 11 time of mirth; 2: 13, jewels. He promises to save Judah and after his anger turns he promises to defeat Israel's foes, but by His power and not their's. In what are we to look for the fulfillment of these predictions of blessings? They were partially fulfilled before Christ. When some of the Israelites were mingled with the tribe of Judah in the return under Zerubbabel they never relapsed into idolatry, 2 Chron. 10: 17; 11: 13-16. This blending began before the captivity by emigration. It is further asserted that the ten tribes were carried into the same land, into which Judah was subsequently carried—Babylon. Mention is particularly made of Levi, Benjamin, Ephraim, and Manasseh being with Judah in settling Jerusalem, I Chron. 9: 2, 3. After return from exile they are repeatedly called Israel, Rom. 9: 6; 11: 26; Ezra 2: 70; 6: 16, 17. The twelve tribes are recognized in the N. T., Acts 26: 7. Paul was of the tribe of Benjamin, Phil. 3: 5; Anna, tribe of Asher, Luke 2: 36. While here are incipient and partial fulfillments, we do not find what corresponds particularly and directly to the terms of the predictions. There was no multitude, as predicted, no complete conversion to God, no inalienable possession of God's favor.

divinely appointed for its accomplishment.
Partially fulfilled before Coming of Xst.
Return of Zerubabbel — Blessing c time r
2 Chron 10:15   31::14 6

By rainfall   Lev 7:31 & 36
3to   3:1 70

The entire body of Israel was not united to Judah. Zerubbabel was not king, and all Israel do not return. As inadequately met before the coming of Christ, we must look for the residue since his coming. **IV. Representative Period.**—3: 4; 2: 5. Service to Baal 2: 17. These crimes (to Baal) are the only ones charged. 2 Kings 10: 28, Jehu destroyed Baal out of Israel. 2 Kings 12: 14. Hosea 8: 10-14, we see that it took form of worshipping golden calves. 13: 1, 2 shows that they thought worship of God was same as that of Baal for when the people return they shall not call him Baalim.

Fulfilment of Blessings is explained in two ways. (*a*) The lineal descendants of the patriarchs, Israel; (*b*) the spiritual seed, those who are successors to the privileges of Israel. If we adopt the former, the substance of the prediction is that the lineal descendants will be as numerous as the sands of the sea, be converted to God, and made His people. The theocratic king of the house of David will be Christ on an earthly throne; thus the prediction becomes a wholly national one, only applied to the ten tribes, or, at most, to the descendants of Jacob. Any other application is subversive of any real intent. According to the other view the descendants of Israel are to be counted not in the lineal descent of the tribes, but in a spiritual succession. **Spiritual succession** is urged:

1. Israel as God's people, and in the sense of the promise never was co-extensive with Abraham's natural posterity. Some excluded, others outside included. Ishmael and the sons of Keturah cut off. The descent was counted in the line of Isaac, Esau was cut off, and the line counted from Jacob. A provision was made at the same time to give the seal of circumcision to those in the house of Abraham. In every period in the history of God's people has this been the case, Ex. 12: 48-49. Multiplication in Egypt a mixed multitude, Ex. 12: 49. Strangers as those born in the land, at the same time those who violated the covenant were cut off from the people, Gen. 17: 14. This excision might occur on a large or small scale, might affect individuals or whole nations. Ex. 1: 10—the ten tribes rejected. 2 Kings 17: 18. God was angry with Israel. When Christ came, another great excision occurred: those who received Christ were called the true Israel, all others being apostates. It was the faithful few who inherited the promises, and at the same time their numbers were increased by believing Gen-

tiles, and thus the continuity was preserved. God did not have one people under the O. T., and another under the N. T., not one church then, and another now. It was Israel then and Israel still, by a regular succession. Israel was a church as well as a nation, and the promises were to Israel as a church. In the light of the history of the case, believers are those to whom the promises were made, and the church of the O. T. continued in that of the N. T.

2. The abundant and explicit testimony of the N. T. favors this view, John 8: 39: Gal. 3: 7; 3: 28, 29; Rom. 2: 28, 29; 4: 11, 12: 9: 6, 8; Rom. 11 argues at length this view in the grafting in of the Gentile branch to the original olive tree, and the ultimate conversion of the original tree; Eph. 2: 12–20; Rev. 2: 9; 3: 9. These are the most striking representations that believers in Christ constitute the true people of God.

3. That this was the view taken by the apostles, and by them made current in the early church, may be confirmed in this: that if the Jewish converts were heirs of anything particular in the church, they would not be blended with others. If the promises had been exclusively to the descendants of the patriarchs as such, they would not have been permitted to blend with Gentiles. There would then have been a distinction between Gentile and Jewish church.

4. This distinction not having been maintained between Gentile and Jewish converts, it would now lead to a most singular anomaly to claim that the Jews are to receive honor above the gentiles, for if that be so the descendants of the Jews who rejected the Messiah when he came are to be exalted above those who accepted him, for only the former can be recognized, as the latter are lost in their union with the gentiles.

5. The very predictions of H. now in question are applied by two apostles to believing Gentiles: Paul in Rom. 9: 25, 26: Peter in 1 Pet. 2: 9, 10. Thus applied by the apostle of the uncircumcision and the apostle of the circumcision. Other arguments tending to the same conclusion will be raised in taking up other prophets.

Conclusion.—The Christian church, considered as a body of believers, is the heir of the promises, and it is to the church that the promises are to be fulfilled. This is not expecting a promise to be fulfilled to one when made to another. Nor is it taking a promise in one sense, and then using it in another, but Israel, in the Bible sense, is the

Epse 47:22-23

Laws of Cohabitation = between o their seed
+ Cohabitn q it Ew. it Same.
To do a a ch that the Marriages
made not as a matin —

maternal descendants

Christian church. How are we to expect these promises to be fulfilled? Ans.—In a form appropriate to N. T. dispensation. This would modify the meaning so as to make the healing of the schism—the unity of the church, and the return—return to the circle of God's favor. This is what the Holy Ghost intended in the promises. This is the strict meaning, Israel of the promise are the people of God, for (a) true believers are to be as numerous as the sands of the sea; (b) they are united under one head; they should be brought back to Canaan.

Objected:—Threatenings of II. against Israel are taken literally, as against lineal descendants, while promises are taken spiritually, as to the spiritual seed. But the church was then as always made up of two classes. Threatenings were directed vs. unbelievers, in which believers might be involved; promises were to believers, by which unbelievers might be indirectly benefitted; as far as these were accomplished under O. T. dispensation, they were accomplished in a form appropriate to O. T.; as far as they remained to be accomplished, they will be accomplished in form of N. T. So as fulfilled under O. T., they were fulfilled literally, both threatenings and promises.

Have the lineal descendants then no part? Yes, but not as Jews, but as believers in Christ. As to literal return to Canaan: (1) Restoration of the Ten Tribes at least improbable. They cannot be any longer identified. (2) As to the Jews, the N. T. predicts their conversion, but not their return to Palestine. All the O. T. prophets who seem to prophesy a return can be explained like Hosea. (3) It is remarkable, on the other hand, that the Jewish people have been preserved distinct, and the land can now accommodate them. We must, however, suspend our judgment until the event. All prophecies can be explained without this supposition; but if it should occur, it would not involve any inconsistency.

Critical Attacks upon Hosea.—Kuenen School. Hosea gives a vivid picture of the prevalence of sin and corruption in the land, and is open in his denunciation of it, especially of idolatry. On this critics base their attack, and say idolatry was the primitive worship in Israel, and that Hosea here attempts a revolution. And as all previous books imply a pure form of religion, they must belong to a later period, and be not what they claim to be, but spurious. Ans.—(1) By showing the evidence which these previous books afford of their own genuineness. (2) By showing evidence which Hosea affords as to their genuineness. (*a*) Hosea charges the people with apostasy. (*b*) Contains many allusions to Pentateuch as a recognized authority. But Kuenen says that *Torah* of which Hosea speaks instruction, *i. e.*, his own preaching, or a collection of laws, but not Pentateuch. We therefore can argue nothing as to his knowledge of the Pentateuch. Ans.—But *Torah* uniformly—Pentateuch, and the Pentateuch as a written law. Ch. 8 : 12.

Kuenen says again, H. condemns the people's religion because it involved human sacrifice, not because it was idolatry. He might have approved of idolatry as the national religion. Ans.—This is based on a false rendering of 13 : 2, and beyond this has no foundation. Objected : The quotations in N. T. from O. T. have been claimed as showing the impossibility of N. T. inspiration. Hos. 11 : 1 in Matt. 2 : 15. In H. this refers to the exodus of Israel, therefore Matt. is uninspired. Ans.—Meaning of H. clear. Matt. in applying this to Christ must have known what the prophet meant. It is explained not as a new application—too definite,—but as referred to Israel typically. Israel was beloved of God and beset by foes; so was Jesus.

AMOS.

The prophet Amos was by some early fathers confounded with Amoz, the father of Isaiah. This mistake arose from the two words being alike in the Greek. They are altogether different in the Hebrew. Amos means burden ; Amoz means strength. He was taken from the herdsmen of Tekoah, twelve Roman miles from Jerusalem, six miles south of Bethlehem. 2 Chron. 20 : 20. The word "herdsman" is applied to the king of Moab as the owner of flocks, 2 Kings 3 : 4. Was Amos an owner of sheep, or a tender of flocks belonging to others ? We learn that he did not own them from 7 : 14, 15. Thus his occupation as a herdsman is put on a level with his gathering of sycamore fruit. But this latter occupation belonged to poorer people. Further, he says he was not a prophet—nor his previous vocation, not the son of a prophet, *i. e.*, he had not been taught in the schools of the prophets under Elijah, Elisha, etc. It would seem that he was sent on this single errand to Israel from Judah, and this may have been the whole of his ministry.

Time.—The time of the delivery of this message is seen in 1:1. Compare 1 Kings 13:1. The time is still further defined by saying it was two years before the earthquake. Zechariah speaks of it, 14:5, the beginning of threatening judgments. But this does not aid us, for we do not know when it took place. Prove however that his prophecy was not committed to writing immediately upon its delivery. Since he could not have dated his ministry with reference to an event still future.

Divisions.—Chs. 1-6, literal; 7-9, allegorical. Amos consists of three parts according to subject. The three parts are: (*a*) ch. 1:2; 2:5, introductory; (*b*) 2:6; 9:10, denunciatory; (*c*) 9:11—15, promissory.

Theme.—The theme is announced in 1:2, a sentence partly taken from Joel 3:16. (*a*) He does so first in a preliminary denunciation of seven nations in succession. Six contiguous Gentile nations, Syria, Philistia, Tyre, Edom, Ammon, Moab, and finally Judah. The judgments are successive stanzas of like construction, suggesting argument *a fortiori*. If these heathen nations are to be punished, how much more Israel. The heathen are generally contemplated as the foes of Israel; in Amos it is different. Also, if Judah is punished, how much more Israel. These denunciations are embraced in seven stanzas of precisely the same structure, opened and concluded in same way.

The sins against the nations are offenses against the theocracy. In the case of Judah the sin is different. The highest offense is violation of God's law. Gentiles *vs.* the maltreatment of God's people. The only exception, if it be such, is the charge in 2:1, against Moab—offense against the Gentiles. Edom's bones burned into lime is the only exception, if it is offences against covenant people. Because probably at this time Edom was a subject or ally of Judah. (*b*) Then follows the main portion of the book, the denunciation against Israel. After four chapters of literal, it is presented in the form of five symbolic visions. The five are to represent not as many distinct judgments, but are to be taken together as the same judgment in different figures.

Visions.—**1.** The first vision, 7:1-3, presents the instruments of judgments, under the symbol of devouring locusts, being the symbol of foreign foes, even the idea of returning prosperity devoured.

2 The second sets forth the source of these judgments, 7:4-7. It is a devouring fire, symbolical of God's devouring wrath, twice withheld by God's mercy.

3. The third vision, 7 : 7–9, exhibits the character of the judgments, righteous retribution. A plumb-line is seen, and all that is not perpendicular is thrown down. This is the test of their uprightness. Here the prophet is interrupted by Amaziah, the priest of Bethel, forbidding him to prophesy any longer, and telling him to leave the country. He then resumes the series of his visions in the 8th chapter.

4. The fourth vision, 8 : 1–3, is intended to represent the near approach of judgments. The prophet sees a basket of summer fruit, and Israel is shown to be ripe for judgment. It is more expressive in the Hebrew on account of the sound of the vowels.

5. Then the last vision, 9 : 1, the actual infliction of judgment. The Lord is seen standing by the altar of idolatry, and striking down and slaying. The idol is helpless to deliver. Hengstenberg makes this altar—that at Jerusalem. No ground for this. Rather from the connection (8 : 14) the altar at Bethel, which is denounced in other parts of the book (3 : 14; 4 : 4,) and by another man of God sent to Jeroboam I. (1 Kings 13 : 1.)

The main lessons taught by Amos are identical with those taught by Hosea.

Nearer Predictions.—(*a*) 7 : 9. The house of Jeroboam shall perish by the sword : fulfilled in 2 Kings 15 : 10, his son killed after a reign of six months.

(*b*) He predicts further the destruction of the kingdom, the desolation of the land, and the exile of the people, which was fulfilled after the partial deportation by Tiglath-Pileser, was completed by Shalmaneser, king of Assyria, 2 Kings 17 : 6. This occupies the main body of the book.

(*c*) 6 : 9–10. Account of great siege. As regards the fulfillment of this we have no means of knowing, but from 2 Kings 17 : 5, we learn that the siege lasted three years; and 2 Kings 6 : 6–24, shows the great distress of Samaria, famine and pestilence, on a former occasion.

(*d*) Predicts that the sons and daughters of Amaziah shall fall by the sword, and he himself die in exile. Of this we have no further account—no means of knowing whether the prediction was actually fulfilled—no history on the matter.

(*e*) The special predictions of desolation to Israel, 3 : 14; visits to altars of Bethel, 3 : 14; 5 : 5; Gilgal, 7 : 9; *cf.* 2 Kings 13 : 10–15.

More Remote Predictions. 9 : 11–15.—Promissory portion told at the close of denunciation : 9 : 8, 9, that the exile and dispersion would not be a total destruction of the people, but should be a sifting, so as to effect a separation between the good and bad; the good are to remain. The fallen and ruined tabernacle of David should be raised up, repaired and restored, 9 : 11. This means David and his royal house shall be restored to former splendor, 2 : 5. The fall of Judah is presupposed. That it is spoken of as fallen is not sufficiently explained in that in his time the rule diminished from twelve tribes to Judah, but that it should include the fall of Judah also, and should entirely fall before the coming of Christ. This was fulfilled in the fall of the royal line, after the Babylonish captivity. The house of David ceased to be royal, and was reduced to a private condition, but in Christ this kingdom has been restored. The tabernacle of David has been set up in Christ more glorious than ever.

Again, Amos predicts that its sway shall extend over Edom, and all the heathen which are called by the name of the Lord, 9 : 12. This cannot mean only those nations which David had overcome, for this would merely mean that the limits of the restored kingdom would be as extensive as previously. No instance can be adduced of an application of this name to any heathen nation because it was tributary to Judah or subject to it, but applied to the covenant people of God, Deut. 28 : 10. "Called by the name of the Lord," wherever used, is applied to the covenant people of God, 2 Chron. 7 : 14; Dan. 9 : 18, 19; Jer. 14 : 9. In conformity with this usage, the meaning here must be that the re-created kingdom shall bear sway over Edom and other heathen nations, which shall in consequence become a part of the covenant people. They shall thenceforth be called by the name of the Lord. The conquest, from this description of it, must not be by force of arms, but conquered in a spiritual sense. This, therefore, is a prophecy of the calling of the Gentiles. As such is quoted in Acts 15 : 15–17.

Further, he predicts the permanent restoration of Israel out of captivity to their own land, 9 : 13–15, and never to be removed from it again. This must be as parallel in Hosea, partly fulfilled in the return from exile. The O. T. forms must be replaced by N. T. corresponding things. The rest was fulfilled in Christ. It will thus be seen that Hosea and Amos agree entirely in predictions of the proximate future or Messianic period. They predict the fall of the house of Jeroboam though then so strong, and the utter destruction of the kingdom of the ten tribes. Amos does not mention Assyria as the instrument of judgment, which Hosea does, but he threatens captivity to both Israel and Judah, by a nation to be raised up, 6: 14. This captivity is to be a distinct one beyond Damascus, 5: 27.

Special Predictions.—That the smaller kingdoms in the vicinity of Israel should be desolated, direful mortality, etc. In regard to Messianic periods Hosea and Amos agree in a spiritual sense. They predict permanent restoration. They shall be united and governed under the son of David. Amos goes beyond Hosea. (*a*) In showing the prostrate condition of the family of David; (*b*) the announcement in express terms of the calling of the Gentiles, which we have seen is implicitly set forth in Hosea; (*c*) in clear statement that nothing was to be hoped for by ten tribes except in connection with Judah.

Genuineness and truth of Pentateuch found in Amos shown not only in the existence of Pent., but that it was believed by people of Israel and those about them. The political institutions we find here were framed from Pentateuch. In Amos is fact of Pentateuch 4: 11; 1: 11. Edom as Israel's brother as in Gen. 16: 26; 31: 33, &c.

JONAH.

Son of Amittai, 1: 1. Native of Gath-Heepher, 2 Kings 14: 2-5. Which was in the bounds of Zebulon, Josh. 19: 13. Tarshish, a Phœnician settlement in the south of Spain. Jerome says Gath-Heepher was two miles from Sephoris on the way to Tiberias.

Date.—Only data accessible are obtained from the following considerations. (*a*) 2 Kings 14: 25. Israel's enlargement by Jeroboam was said to be in fulfillment of Jonah's prophecy, therefore Jonah prophesied upon close of Jeroboam's reign. (*b*) Position among minor prophets in the canon. It comes after Amos, who prophesied in later years of Jeroboam's reign. So Jonah must have begun to prophesy near the close of J's reign. But it comes before Micah, who prophesied in reign of Jotham, therefore the greater part of his ministry must have come before this time. (*c*) Date of the first invasion of Israel was in reign of Mena-

hem, 2 Kings, 15 : 19. J's mission to Nineveh was for the warning of Israel. Therefore as this invasion was the first assumption of a threatening attitude on part of Assyria, a time *after* this invasion would be a proper time for this mission. A few months of reign and twelve years of interregnum are required by the chronology of the two kingdoms after Jeroboam. We, therefore, argue that 2 Kings 14 : 25, and the book of Jonah were at different periods.

Divisions.—(1) Chaps. 1, 2, first mission, (Mercy.) (2) Chaps. 3, 4, second mission.

Contents.—Extraordinary nature of some of the events has occasioned critical attacks. Abarband: whole account of the fish was a dream of Jonah's while he was sleeping in the side of vessel. Clericus: and by a vessel with figurehead of a whale. Vanderhart: whole narrative a mere allegory. Others: a moral fiction conveying a lesson; a popular legend with an historical basis; a heathen myth, without any historical basis. We have no reason to believe it is not historical. (*a*) The whale is the great stumbling-block. But while the miracle is peculiar, it is no more difficult than any other miracle.

Objected : No whales in the Mediterranean, and if there were their mouth is too small to swallow a man whole.

Ans.—The species of fish is not defined. Heb. LXX. Vulgate—" great fish." Modern interpreters hold it to have been a species of shark, white, soft, long, which are known to have swallowed men whole. (*b*) Repentance of Ninevites incredible, and no mention of it by profane historians. *Ans.*—(1) Apart from Spirit of God there was great incentive. The Assyrians were greatly superstitious and would be likely moved by the appearance among them of a strange prophet, from a foreign country of whose wonderful deliverance they may have heard. (2) The condition of the empire, defeat of their armies may have predisposed them to listen to the warning message. (3) It is not mentioned by profane historians because they had no Assyrian records for it. There were no records because it was too evanescent, and because such events are not recorded. (*c*) Covering of beasts with sackcloth improbable. *Ans.*—We learn from Herodotus that it was a custom to make animals participate in their religious observances, *e. g.*, shaving hair from horses for religious rejoicing. (*d*) Various myths have been proposed as substitutes for the history. But (1) they had no resemblance to the narrative. Oanes, half man and half fish. Resemblance merely in name. Andromeda, chained to rock; delivered by Perseus. Resemblance merely in fact that A. was exposed to a sea-monster. The oldest form is Hesione chained to a rock. In 2nd century, A. D., was said she was swallowed by a fish, and 5th century, A. D., was added that she was disgorged. This shows how legends grow with the form of history. (2) The Jews never adopted such myths. (3) If they had they would have shaped this more to suit their national prejudices.

Positive Arguments in Favor of Historical Character.—(*a*) Natural, obvious interpretation of the language. (*b*) Admission into the canon. (*c*) Authority of the N. T., especially Christ's specific reference to Jonah as a type of himself. Although of a genuine historical character, the narrative is not given as mere history, but for the spiritual lessons which it contains. This is proved: (1) Comparatively small part of the book is occupied with historical occurrences, and a moral lesson is implied in all that are related. (2) Position in the canon—being among the prophetic books, though not itself prophetic. If it had been mere history it would have been classed among the historical books, *e. g.*, Samuel. It is put among prophetic books because the events recorded are typical. (3) Character of his mission. Designed not so much to secure repentance of Nineveh, nor as a promise to Gentiles, as a lesson to Israel, *cf.* Jer. 27: 2, 3 *f.* (4) No attempt at permanent result, as in cases of Elijah and Christ with the Gentiles. (5) Testimony of Christ, who calls attention to the spiritual lessons of this book. Matt. 16: 24.

Lesson of this Book.—(1) A means by which other prophets may justify themselves when their predictions fail, Hitzig. This is purely skeptical, based upon failure of prophecy. (2) Salvation was to be by penitence and pious feeling. *e. g.* Sailors, Jonah. Ninevites repented and were saved. (3) Narrowness of the Jews. Jehovah was God of Gentiles also To understand this we must see what were the motives of Jonah's action, Fairbairn. If God should overthrow N. for its sins, this would be a striking instance of his justice, and would lead Israel to repentance. J. desires this, but fearing God's mercy would save it, he fled. Jewish tradition, more concerned for his country (Son) than for his God. (Father.) Others find a motive in diffidence; risk of the undertaking, hopelessness of the task. True view: J. feared to preach to N. lest it should be spared for

∴ Contrary to use analogy.
No harm wh. cd not be proved a fable on such grounds as above urged.

Pl. Nealis story hath, joined with Curse on Queen of Sheba.

1/ only ... things narrated wh. bear on the purpose

Elisha sent to Damascus 1 Kings 19:15 2 Kings 8:7 f. not so much for ... as to raise up a ... for God. Curious almost parallel to Jonah.

Mt 12:39-40 Lk 11:29-30

2/ Ewald.
3/ Bleek, Hengstenberg.
Fairbairn suggests moral motive but not satisfactory.
4:2 ... reason given by prophet himself.

Deut 30:1-3

Ezra 3:1-7
 Mat 12:41
Dec 4:20—
the acts of Jeroboam — did not cause
further reaction at that time.

Mat 12:40
 Ln 11:30

If my thesis be true as scale as possn so
far for all events at records — some any.
Buy capt. after + Maccab.

the overthrow of Israel. He desires to die after the repentance of the city, because he felt that the doom of his country was sealed. *cf.* Elijah at Carmel.

Symbolic events show Gentiles less obdurate than Israel. Twofold application. (*a*) Admonitory—of the present. J. cast into the sea for his disobedience; mariners cry to God and are saved. Israel had many prophets, yet had not repented. N. repents at the preaching of one. (*b*) Typical. J. cast out of ship, afterwards delivered; Jews rejected, though not utterly destroyed. J. preaches to Gentile Nineveh, who repents. Word of God will be preached to Gentiles who repent. Plainly stated, Amos 9:12. Same truth taught elsewhere in Scripture. Elijah was sent to widow of Zarepta, 1 Kings 17. Elisha cures Naaman, 2 Kings 5. Christ preaches to woman of Samaria, John 4. Syrophœnician woman's daughter healed, Mark 7. Magi at the Saviour's birth. Christ unfolds a still deeper typical meaning in Jonah's being in the belly of the fish. Typical of His death and burial. Not merely as to length of time; but the apparent destruction of Jonah was not end of his work. It only paves the way for his miraculus deliverance and preaching to the Ninevites. Same fact is apparently used in Rom: 11:15.

Date of Composition.—Various views. Assyrian exile. Time of king Josiah. Time of Maccabees. Those who held to mythical origin place it as far as possible from time of Prophets. This class argue (*a*) J. not the author because he is spoken of in third person. This is the case in books of undoubted authorship. (*b*) Numerous Aramaisms. No more than in Hosea, whose date is acknowledged. (*c*) Prayer of Jonah said to be inappropriate is taken from Psalms written after exile. We may claim as well that Psalms were composed from J's prayer. It is urged that it is inappropriate to condition in which J. was, therefore was not written by Jonah. *Ans.*— (1) No argument. For whoever wrote the book must have thought it appropriate or he would not have inserted it, and J. may have erred in this matter as well as another. (2) It is appropriate, since he had reason to be thankful for his deliverance from the sea. (3) It is natural that he should base his prayer on Scripture, adapting figurative language of others to his own real sufferings. (*d*) Use of past tense in description of Nineveh, implying city not in existence when book was written. But it merely implies what it was when J. found it, and ch. 4:11, God spared N. (*e*) Impossible size of city. *Ans.*—Measurements of ancient historians agree with Jonah's. Modern historians differ. Layard agrees with Jonah. "Three days' journey"—circuit of city. Rawlinson thinks it means sum of lengths of all the streets. Far-fetched. Not necessary to suppose all property occupied with residences.

Authorship of Jonah Proved.—(*a*) The introduction is such as a prophet would claim for himself. This is a presumption in favor of its being production by Jonah. (*b*) It is claimed for Jonah, 1 : 1. (*c*) Placed among prophetic books. Its position is testimony of the collectors that it was the production of Jonah, and the later the date of the writing the less danger of mistake. (*d*) Hatred by Jews for Gentiles makes its production at a late date impossible. (*e*) Tradition favors authorship of Jonah.

ASSYRIAN PERIOD.

II.—PROPHETS OF JUDAH.

Condition of the Kingdom. It was not schismatic. Idolatry was introduced by the daughter of Ahab. The reaction comes in more completely under Joash than under Jehu in Jeremiah. There were four princes in this period. The first and second were godly; Ahaz, idolatrous; Hezekiah, reformer. Evil was at no time totally eradicated. Inflictions by Syria and Assyria.

There are five prophets in this period: Joel, Obadiah, Isaiah, Micah, Nahum, and this is their chronological order. There was conflict all the time between evil tendencies of the people and influences of the good kings. The people being thus balanced, God employed both mercy and judgment. In first reigns, mercy; but the people became proud; then judgment, but Judah being not yet ripe for overthrow was spared. Their ministers differ from those of their contemporaries in Israel.

Nature of Their Ministry.—1. They are ministers of gentleness rather than severity; of hope, rather than denunciation. They are either positive or negative. Micah, positive; Obadiah, Nahum, negative; Joel, Isaiah, both. The *positive* give greater space to promise, and make these of a larger and fuller kind than in Israel. Exactly one-half

of Joel is promissory; and Isaiah, in the last twenty-seven chapters, devotes himself expressly to the work of comfort; Micah gives large space to promise. The contrast of this period with Israel is great. In Judah, the promises made are not all left to the distant future, but include present deliverances. The *negative* are consolatory. Denunciation and downfall of their heathen foes, because the overthrow of these is mercy to Judah. Their overthrow is in order that the power may be given to Israel. The heathen for a time will overthrow the people of God, but it is added that they shall ultimately be cast down, and the power given to God's people. This is so in regard to Edom in Obadiah. Nahum tells of a similar judgment on Nineveh and Assyria. Isaiah against Assyria and Babylon.

2. The greater clemency of the Lord to Judah is shown by granting to the prophets of the kingdom a range of much greater foresight than to Israel. Not only do they advise them of the events immediately before them, but they also disclose the remote future, preparing the people in advance for remote necessities. (*a*) A most appalling disaster to Judah in the succeeding period. (*b*) Existence of Judah not limited to this period, but continued. (*c*) Judah is to be brought into contact with the greatest nations of the world, and is to experience their hostility. (*d*) Needful for prophetic marks of the Messiah to be given. For these reasons a much greater range is given to Judah than to Israel. The overthrow of the ten tribes and its attending circumstances are almost the whole that is given to Israel. To Judah, in addition: A series of successive judgments against Judah; Assyrian invasion, and its failure; captivity of Babylon and its deliverance; overthrow of Nineveh; judgments against inferior foes; and, lastly, the overthrow of Babylon herself, the foe of the future.

The body of the revelations just given has been variously apportioned. *Joel:* A general overthrow of the future, without distinctly specifying the events in it. Judah has repeated strokes of judgment, and when it is brought to itself by this means, God shall return to it, and execute judgments upon its enemies. This is filled up more in detail by other prophets. *Micah* dwells exclusively upon the fortunes of God's people, their punishment for unfaithfulness, and their subsequent blessedness. *Obadiah* and *Nahum* individualize the work of judgment upon the foes of God's people. Obadiah tells of the fate of Edom, the hereditary foe of Judah.

Nahum, toward the close of this period, foretells the downfall of Nineveh. *Isaiah* goes over the ground in a general way marked out by *Joel*, but differs from him in unfolding in their details what Joel gives in general outline, while at the same time he goes beyond in the fullness of the blessings of God's people. *Micah:* The judgments against the foes exceeds Obadiah and Nahum. To no one is so large a view of the future given as to Isaiah, until the time of Daniel.

Messianic Predictions.—The range of the Messianic predictions of the Judean prophets is also extensive. In Israel it was negative. Judah does this, but goes far beyond this position. The people shall not only return to God from their apostasy, as Amos says, but they shall also be purged. All their foes shall themselves be humbled and destroyed, all that is noxious in animal creation—even death itself. No form of evil shall remain to the people of God. The prophets of Judah are not confined to this negative view of the case. They develop the positive beauties of the period, as to the people of God and the Gentiles.

1. The people of God, both in inward character and outward condition, shall correspond to what they should be. They shall be holy in their character, and have the Spirit of God poured out upon them, and then their kingdom of peace shall be universal, perpetually prosperous, and shall sway the whole world, whose resources shall flow into it, and contribute to its honor.

2. The calling of the Gentiles, and their conversion to God, are more clearly revealed than in Israel. It was shadowed forth by Jonah, stated limitedly by Amos, but by the prophets of Judah in the most unambiguous way. "All nations will flock to God, etc."

Person of Christ.—Besides this general development of the characteristics of the Messianic period as respects the people of God and the Gentiles, the Judean prophets bring into view the Person of the Messiah as was not done by the prophets of Israel. The prophets of Israel predicted the family of David, and its rise again, but do not view the Person of Christ. The prophets of Judah say he shall appear during a time of oppression, and shall spring from the house of David, born in Bethlehem, the son of a virgin. He shall honor Galilee, be rejected by the Jews, but accepted by the Gentiles. By his death, he shall be brought into glory, and establish a kingdom of righteousness. Obadiah and Nahum simply refer to the Messianic period, the former explicitly,

the latter implicitly. They simply refer to it in its negative phase, as to its deliverance from and judgments upon the foes of God's people. Isaiah and Micah, between whom there is a close connection, speak of the Person of the Messiah, of his birth in Bethlehem, of his deity, and of his kingly office as Messiah. Isaiah alone gives the birth from the virgin, the sufferings and vicarious death. The blessings are nowhere set forth so well and so gloriously as in Isaiah.

Divisions.—This prophetic period, though strictly a unit, may be divided into two portions: (*a*) Outward prosperity under the vigorous reign of the pious Uzziah, and before the Assyrians had come. (*b*) Trial under Ahaz and Hezekiah. This is after the invasion by Syria and Ephraim, and when the Syrians present a threatening aspect. To the first, belong Joel, Obadiah, and the first six chapters of Isaiah. The prophets endeavor to break the proud spirit of the people, which prosperity had engendered, by setting forth the coming trials. To the second, belong Micah, Nahum, and considerable of the remainder of Isaiah. Here the downfall of Nineveh, and the Messiah as defender and king of his people, are displayed. Isaiah's ministry extends not only through both portions of this period, but goes beyond the downfall of Sennacherib, and proposes the way for the next period, the Chaldean. These prophets of Judah in the Assyrian period may be compared in minor points:

Personal and Family Relations.—Mention is made of the fathers of Joel and Isaiah; the residences of Micah and Nahum are given; but of Obadiah, only the name. This is all we have of their personal history, except a few scraps of Isaiah's. Probably all except Nahum belonged to Judah.

Duration of Ministry.—Isaiah under four kings; Micah under three kings. The ministries of Joel, Obadiah, and Nahum were probably brief.

Structure of the Books.—Isaiah in successive portions, which are kept distinct; Micah, a general summary of the revelations made to him, without distinction of date. The other prophets have done the same, unless, as seems to be the case with Obadiah and Nahum, they have given us only a single discourse.

JOEL.

From 1:9, 13, 14, some infer that he was of Levitical descent. There is no warrant for this.

Date of His Ministry is shown by his position between Hosea and Amos. He must, therefore, have been of the time of Uzziah, and during the part when Jeroboam, king of Israel, was yet living. For Hosea's ministry began in that part of Uzziah's reign when Jeroboam was living, and the ministry of Amos was begun and finished during same period. So anything between these ministries must also have been in that same period. Some put him at a still earlier date, as far back as Joash. The enemies given as enemies of Judah can all be shown to have been enemies in the time of Joash. This proves nothing, because the powers mentioned were hereditary foes, and ready for war at any time. Amos denounces the same nations, and accuses them of the same crimes. Others place Joel at a later date than Hezekiah. This is claimed from 3:2, but the "Israel" mentioned there means both branches of the covenant people, and their captivity is future, and not spoken of as past. Further, Joel must have preceded Amos, since A. begins with words with which J. closes and the way in which they appear in the two books shows that A. is one who quotes. But A. finished his ministry before that captivity, so J'.s could not have been after it.

Divisions.—There are two parts, of 36 vs. each: *a* 1:2; 2:17, the judgment and exhortation to repentance. *b* 2:18; 3:21, the blessing. *A* is a description of unexampled distress and scourge of devouring insects. Is it allegorical or real? Whichever they were, they were symbolical of the punishment to Judah by invading enemies. Some say there is an allusion to the four great powers of the ancient world, by which the people of God were successively assailed. *B* In the second, we pass from judgment to mercy. (*a*) Removal of scourge. (2:18-27.) (*b*) Bestowment of all spiritual gifts. (2:27-32.) (*c*) Utter destruction of all foes. Ch. 3. Many critics think Joel wrote more than we have, and they think they find it in Isaiah. Joel quoted Matt. 24:29. Rom 10:13 equals Joel 2:32. Rev. 14:15 equals Joel 3:13.

The first part is a description of unparalleled distress by a swarm of insects. There are different views as to what kind of insects is intended, four terms being employed. (*a*) They denote four kinds of locusts; (*b*) Different species of the same kind; (*c*) The same insect in successive stages of its growth. Four stages of growth. Credner: "*Gazam* is the migratory locust, which visits Palestine chiefly in the

autumn, '*arbeh*, the young brood, *yeleg*, the young locust in the last stage of its transformation, or before changing its skin for the fourth time, and *chasil*, the perfect locust after this last change, so that, as the brood sprang from the *gazam*, *chasil* would be equivalent to *gazam*." (See Keil, "Minor Prophets," Joel 1 : 1–4.) Palestine was first visited by the locusts in the autumn, full grown; this swarm laid its eggs and perished in the Red Sea. The combined heat and drought favored the hatching of the eggs in the spring. Then describes a running or climbing. They have to cast the skin four times before they come out perfect. Objections to this view: (*a*) It requires an interpolation of the laying the eggs, and hatching, and requires a different subject. (*b*) While assuming distinct significance for three, four is a species. This theory has been modified. But the only proof that there would then be successive stages, is (1) that in verse 4 they occur in a particular order; but in 2 : 25, they occur in another order. (2) '*Arbeh* is not so used elsewhere, but is the usual term for locust. (3) *Yeleg* cannot have this meaning, because Nahum 3 : 6, makes it mean "full-grown." (4) In Ps. 105 : 34, '*arbeh* and *yeleg* are synonomous: so also '*arbeh* and *chasil* in Ps. 78 : 46. *Chasil*, Deut. 28 : 38, expresses the act of devouring. On the whole it is best to consider them as poetic equivalents of the same thing. The terms used really mean "gnawer," "swarmer," "feeder," "devourer."

Do they mean actual locusts, or are they symbolic? Doubtless the latter, because: **1.** They are a natural figure for hostile invaders; *cf.* Rev 9 : 3–11, and often in SS. **2.** It is represented as a judgment of unparalleled severity, and to be the last before the Messianic blessing shall come. This would be exaggerated if actual locusts were meant. *Cf.* 2 : 2, the darkness was to be before them, not by them, the Lord's hosts 2: 10; 2 : 11. **3.** Their ravages are not past nor present—as they must be on the literal hypothesis, for it is impossible to suppose the prophet would spend so much space in predicting a mere swarm of locusts,—but future. In 3: 15, preterites are used and yet refer to the future, and in 1: 15, "the day of the Lord" is identified with locusts. **4.** The connection of the prophecy demands an allegorical hypothesis. The heathen are denounced for crimes not yet committed. This can only relate to the crime predicted in 3: 7. In consequence of final judgment on the heathen, strangers shall pass through Jerusalem no more, etc. **5.** The attributes of the locusts, and the terms used of them, belong to a nation, as *goy*, 1: 6, and *am*, 2: 2. The latter is twice used of ants, but never the former. They are called "northern," 2: 29; but locusts come from the south, and invasions from Babylon from the north. The reason assigned for destruction is that they have done great things and will be punished. They shall perish in two seas at once, 2: 20, and so mere foes on all sides. 2: 17, priests are to pray God for deliverance, that the heathen should not rule over them, which is not because they are so reduced as to be a prey to the heathen, nor that they should become a by-word among them. 2: 25, speaks of the years the locusts have eaten. 2: 4, 5, they are like horses and chariots, which shows their true meaning. In 1: 19, 20, the figure is changed to that of fire, which shows it to be but a figure. Literalists say it refers to a drought, but it is not said there would be one. **6.** The allegorical view is the oldest, and has also been most prevalent. Targum substitutes names of people for locusts. Rufinus is the only Latin father holding the literal view. Some Jews hold literal view. Bochart finds literal interpretation among Christians, followed by rationalists. It is not necessary that all the names, 1: 12, should have separate signification. It is a question whether the four different names of locusts have different significations. Ephræm Syrus refers them to different invaders. Jerome, Cyril, and Hengstenberg refers them to the four world kingdoms of Daniel, which should oppress Israel. Nothing is certain, except that these are curious coincidences. Ch. 1 has descriptions of judgment; ch. 2 has the same theme, but under different aspects, agents are different, described in vs. 10, 11, 12, etc.; then in v. 18 the tone changes to that of promise. *These promises are:* **1.** Removal of the scourge, and restoration of all that had been lost, 2: 18-27; **2.** Bestowment of spiritual gifts, 2: 28-32; **3.** Destruction of foes, ch. 3. In 2: 23 occurs in the English version an incorrect translation. The correct meaning is "teacher of righteousness." This includes all whom God commissioned to instruct the people, and includes the prophet, and the greatest teacher of all, the Messiah. "Teacher" is used generically. In consequence of the people being thus led to righteousness, God would give them abundant rains in the first "month," as in the A. V., but it should be in the first "place." Observe, **1.** This has the sanction of all the versions. **2.** The usage of the word *moreh* is not rain, but teacher, in

every other passage. In Ps. 84: 7, the meaning is disputed.
3. Expression "to righteousness" favors teacher. If it means rain, it must mean that which is suitable, a sense it never has elsewhere. In A. V., "moderately" should be "to righteousness." **4.** Translation "former rain" would introduce a tautology, for next clause has the same. He pours out upon them a spiritual blessing. This shall be upon all flesh, *i. e.*, not only upon all mankind, without national distinction, but also upon all classes of men, irrespective of age, rank or sex. In Acts 2: 16, Peter tells us the fulfillment of the prophecy had begun then, and also the marvelous outpouring of the Spirit was not a final completion of the prophecy but only a beginning. There were to be signal judgments upon the enemies of God; there were to be premonitory wonders, 2: 30, 31. In ch. 3, we have an account of the judgment itself. This chapter is figurative, but in substance it has met repeated fulfillment, as one after another of the enemies of God has been destroyed, and it shall finally be fulfilled completely in the universal judgment of the world to come. In 3: 2, the scene of judgment is laid in the valley of Jehoshaphat, which is supposed to be the same referred to in 2 Chron. 20: 26. Others suppose from 3: 16 that the valley nearest the temple must be meant, so a Jewish literalism expects the final judgment there. Jehoshaphat, Jehovah judged, hence, "valley of God's judgment." 3: 1–8, charges against the heathen; all nations are represented as leagued against the Lord, and are destroyed by Him. 3: 9–15, all people are called to come and witness and assist in this affliction. 3: 17–21, the blessed results: His people are to be preserved. The type of the abundance is expressed in 3: 18, even the most desolate places shall be blessed. Egypt and Edom are types of the foes of Israel, and they shall be destroyed.

OBADIAH.

Other Obadiahs in the Bible but no identification. 2 Chron. 17: 7; 34: 12. Because his name is nowhere else found they think that is testimony against it but it is the reverse.

Shortest of all O. T. books. Not a fragment. Name borne by others, ministry in Judah, of author's life, duration of ministry, nothing known. **Date of ministry** inferred from position in Minor Prophets. Comes after Amos, whose ministry was in the first part of Uzziah's reign, and before Jonah, whose ministry was ended before the close of Jotham's reign. So O's ministry must have been in latter part of Uzziah's reign or in first part of Jotham's. Some place it as early as reign of Joram. Others as late as in or after the Bab. exile. *First view* as to date *confirmed* (a) perhaps by ver. 20, (b) indefinite allusions to Chaldeans, ver. 11. (c) Denunciations of Edom in same period by Joel, Amos, Isaiah. **Three parts**: vs. 1–9 the desolation to which Edom was doomed, vs. 10–16 reason of it, his unbrotherly treatment of Judah, vs. 17–21 contrasted restoration and enlargement of Israel. **Predictions.** 1. Capture of Jerusalem vs. 11–14. This is the passage in which there is difference of opinion as to date. 2. Hostility then shown by Edom, comp. Ps. 137: 7; Ezek. 35: 5. 3. Overthrow of Edom (a) by the nations, ver. 1 fulfilled by Nebuchadnezzar, comp. Mal. 1: 3, 4; (b) by the house of Jacob restored to their ancient seats, ver. 18. 4. Day of the Lord upon all nations, vs. 15, 16, fulfilled successively and simultaneously. 5. Restoration of Israel, vs. 17–21. Saviour's human champions and the Messiah.

Correspondence with preceding and succeeding prophets, Jeremiah, ch. 49; not (a) independently suggested to both, nor (b) servile imitation, but (c) indication of oneness, (d) mutual sanction, (e) call attention to what is about to pass into accomplishment. Incidental evidence of genuineness and canonicity of earlier Scriptures. Critical extremes, (a) pedantic minuteness and baseless conclusion; (b) alterations of text to restore an imaginary conformity.

ISAIAH.

PRELIMINARY CHAPS. I.–VI.

This prophet is called the "prince of prophets." His writings are the largest and clearest as to the work of the Messiah. Singular fitness in his name. "Isaiah" means "salvation of Jehovah," and such was his message. According to Is. 1: 1, he was the son of Amoz, of whom nothing is known. He lived in Jerusalem, the "middle city," 2 Kings, 20: 4. He was married, and had at least two children, 7:

[illegible handwritten notes]

3; 8 : 3,18. The name of one, Shear-jashub, signifies mercy to Judah, after the first coming judgment. The name of the other, Maher-shalal-hash-baz, signifying speedy ruin to Syria. Some suppose a third son, 7 : 14, Immanuel, but the child thus spoken of is the Messiah. There is no evidence that his wife was inspired; 8 : 3, called prophetess simply from her relation to Isaiah.

Leading Events.—1. Confronting Ahaz, ch. 7. 2. Encouraging Hezekiah, ch. 37. 3. Healing of Hezekiah, 37–39 chs., and reproof of his vain display. Ch. 38 : 21 is quoted in favor of his medical skill, but this is given only in virtue of his prophetic office.

Duration of Ministry.—During the reigns of Uzziah, Hezekiah, Ahaz, Jotham. Not during their entire reigns which would be 113 years. The earliest date in the book, 6 : 1, the year Uzziah died; latest date, 36 : 1. Between these 46 years is the shortest period that can be allowed. Probably his ministry extended some time beyond this. Some say until the time of Manasseh, because (a) Jewish tradition says that surviving Hezekiah, he was sawn asunder by Manasseh. Some refer to Heb. 11 : 37. (b) Refers the rest (2 Chron. 32 : 32), of the acts of Hezekiah to a writing of Isaiah, and this, they say, implies Isaiah survived Hezekiah. (c) A record of Sennacherib's death, Is. 37 : 38. (d) Not forbidden by Isaiah 1 : 1; cf. Jeremiah 1 : 3, Dan. 1 : 21.

Structure of the Book.—1. Utterly confused, jumbled together, disorderly, and some seek to bring them into an order which mangles the book.

2. Partial and orderly collections, receiving accidental accretions, and ultimately blended. This, too, is arbitrary, based on an assumption of disagreements in the book, and on that of the collection of these parts by another than the prophet himself.

3. Chronologically arranged as delivered. In favor of this it is urged that all the dates which *do* occur in the book are in chronological order. The two cases in which a departure is assumed are chs. 1 and 6. Chapter 6, described, it is affirmed, the inauguration of the prophet into office. If this be correct, then ch. 6 is the first of all chronologically. They assume that Isaiah, having put together his prophecies uttered in the reigns of Uzziah and Jotham, appended to them his original commission in order to show them that the denunciations which he had uttered were in strict accordance with the divine command. But in ch. 6 the prophet de-

scribes not his original commission, but a special dedication for a new and specific work. Ch. 1, all suppose to be out of its original place. Not a discourse in the outset of his ministry, but the last of all, and not prepared until the whole was written. It is supposed that this chapter is the introduction prepared at the conclusion of the whole. The decision of the question rests mainly on the interpretation of vs. 7-9, whether the preterite is historical or prophetical. The latter indicates a future event spoken of as having already occurred. The country was not ravaged to the extent there mentioned until the time of Hezekiah. In general, then, the order is chronological.

4. Others insist on a topical arrangement, prophecies relating to the same theme being classed together. Vitringa, as follows: (*a*) chs. 1-12, prophecies relating to Judah and Ephraim, from the earlier part of his ministry. (*b*) 13-23, Relating to other nations. (*c*) 24-35, Punishment of Jews and enemies of the church. (*d*) 36-39, Historical. (*e*) 40-66, Person and reign of Christ. Gesenius divides substantially the same, but joins (*d*) and (*e*) as both relating to the deliverance from the exile.

5. A better view is to combine the chronological order and topical.—A record of his ministry in its leading features as they were successively unfolded, viz.: (*a*) 1-6, Before the Syrian invasion. Exhibition of the certainty and necessity of the coming judgment. The prophecies were delivered to an outwardly prosperous people, under Hezekiah and Jotham. Little space is devoted to promises. All that are given relate to the distant future. Messianic period referred to brings out the present guilt and unfaithfulness. Necessity of judgments to prepare for the blessings of the future. Person of the Messiah only once alluded to, and then only obscurely. (*b*) 7-37, Extending to the Assyrian invasion. Alternate between judgment and mercy. One judgment by Syria already sent, and another by Assyria still in the future. Necessity of a severer judgment in the future. The person of the Messiah appears repeatedly in his kingly office. He is a pledge of his people's preservation and deliverance from oppression. (*c*) 38-66, Subsequent to the Assyrian invasion. The second judgment by Assyria is past, but another more fearful one is yet to come, which shall not merely threaten the destruction of the holy city, but shall actually accomplish it, and they shall be taken away from their land, breaking the presumption of sinners over Sennacherib's destruc-

tion, by this announcement. He yet gives comfort to the pious, who were in danger of despairing, that though this calamity shall befall them, it shall come to an end, and the oppressor shall be overthrown. Cyrus named, Israel named. Here the Messiah is again exhibited, not as a king but as a prophet, and as a sufferer, the head of his people, and identified with them in the accomplishment of that which shall avail for the good of others, but suffering for himself. The last section is adapted to a great necessity of the future, hence not distinct discourses as the preceding, but one connected composition.

Unity of plan in the whole book.

1. Chs. 1-6. The denunciations of the early chapters increase in vehemence, until they culminate in sentence of desolation, by successive judgments pronounced by God himself, in the vision of ch. 6. This is the germ of all that comes after. The prophet is informed that the people instead of being benefited by his ministry would continue in sin until the land should be desolated, although they should not be finally destroyed, because there was still a holy seed which should be preserved. The sixth chapter is in its right place. If this is the place where this vision is to be recorded it is also where it should appear. If we see in 6th ch. only his call to the ministry we lose much of its truth. The previous chapters lead up to the 6th, Jehovah speaks in the 6th ch.

2. Chs. 7-37. Subdivided, (a) 7-12, (b) 13-27, (c) 28-35 (d) 36-37. (a) Prophecies occasioned by the first of the predicted judgments, the invasion by Syria and Ephraim, promising deliverance from this, but threatening a sorer one to come. (b) Meaning of these predicted events to the world at large. (c) Occasioned by the approach of the second judgment, the Assyrian invasion, promising its miraculous defeat. (d) Record of the Assyrian invasion and its overthrow.

3. Chs. 38-66. (a) Chs. 38, 39, occasion of predicting the third judgment. (b) 40-66, comfort in view of this judgment and assurance of ultimate deliverance. This same work, of judgments upon the people for their sins, is spoken of in general terms by Obadiah and Joel. They said it would be carried to the extent of destroying the holy city, but by what steps and foes, was unknown, until Isaiah revealed it. No prophet of this or any other period is explicit except Daniel.

1. Subdivided into ch. 1, chs. 2-4, ch. 5, and ch. 6. Ch. 1, vs. 2-4, charge of ingratitude and sin; vs. 5-9, land to be ravaged in consequence; vs. 10-15, observance of the ritual could not save them; vs. 16-20, sin must be repented of and forsaken; or, vs. 21-31, it shall be wiped out by judgment. Chs. 2-4; (*a*) 2: 2-4, Zion's glorious destiny, as the seat of a worship which shall attract and bless all nations; (*b*) 2: 5; 4: 1, present failure to realize this destiny, which is due to their sins, and shall be remedied by judgments; (*c*) 4: 2-6, Zion shall be thus purged of evil, and rise to her true blessedness and glory; Branch of the Lord and fruit of the earth denotes the Messiah; (*a*) the Branch, Jer. 23: 5; 33: 15; Zech. 3: 8; 6: 12, comp. Isa. 11: 1;*(b*) ancient and common explanation; (*c*) no other satisfactory. Ch. 5, Parable of the vine and its application. Ch. 6, The vision, commission and announcement.

The first period contains four distinct prophecies. In each there is the same idea. They are so many arguments for the necessity of judgment, and of purification, anterior to the Messiah's coming. In the second discourse it is put in the glorious destiny of Zion, and the seat of the true religion. In the third discourse the same truths under the emblem of a vineyard, carefully attended to, and yet it produces wild grapes. In consequence of this the wall of the vineyard is broken down. This prepares the way for the last discourse, ch. 6, in which these denunciations culminate in a sublime vision. The Lord appears in his temple with majesty, and pronounces formal sentence on his people— desolation and banishment, but not of entire destruction. According to the election of grace, a remnant shall be preserved. There is a holy seed to remain.

This idea which is here brought out is really the keynote of the book, and shows reason for its arrangement and structure. All the rest is built upon and grouped around successive judgments. The future has thus far been set forth in its general outline, but by what agents the judgment is to be inflicted, is not yet declared. This majestic vision of ch. 6, was seen in the year king Uzziah died, ch. 6: 1. As Uzziah was a leper during the latter years of his reign, Jotham (2 Chron. 26: 21) was then acting monarch. For the remainder of Jotham's reign, we have no distinct utterances. Whether the prophet was dumb (Ezek. 33: 22) or not, cannot be determined, if new revelation was given him. The king had from his throne pronounced judgment, and

the prophet holds his peace. The decree heard in the temple enters on its first stage in the days of Ahaz. Prophet was sent with message which was constantly disregarded.

2. Chs. 7-37. (A) 7-12. Subdivision of chs. 7-12: (1) Ch. 7, circumstances, deliverance from this invasion, but a severer one from Assyria. (2) 8: 1; 9: 7, Both from this present and that future distress Immanuel is a pledge of protection to them that fear God. (3) 9: 8; 10: 4, Ephraim, the foe of the present, shall perish. (4) 10: 5; 10: 34, Assyria, the foe of the future, shall likewise perish. (5) Ch. 11 and 12, Blessings of Immanuel's reign.

The moment Isaiah met Ahaz was a critical one for Judah, and their unbelief was the immediate cause of the evils which followed. The question was distinctly proposed to them, whether they would rely on God for assistance, or on Assyria. The unfortunate king of the people chose the fatal consequences. The Assyrian general, Rabshakeh (36: 2), stood on the conduit of the upper pool, where Isaiah met Ahaz, and delivered his insulting message. The direful vision of the first chapter is here given. In his discourse to the king, Isaiah (7 ch.) had sketched dark visions of Assyrian invasion, and no relief. Severe chastisement of sins, followed by the overthrow of foes. Such is the future of the people of God. When Isaiah met Ahaz, he delivered the message, 7: 7-9. The sign given was the virgin's child, comp. Ex. 3: 11, 12, time of deliverance indicated, vs. 15, 16. *Almah*, a virgin, (*a*) etymology, (*b*) usage, (*c*) cognate languages, (*d*) LXX. A child miraculously born, (*a*) Mat. 1: 22, 23, (*b*) solemnity of the announcement, (*c*) the name and 8: 8-10, (*d*) 9: 6, 7. Not the prophet's child, (*a*) mother a virgin, (*b*) 8: 1-4. Three views, (*a*) Messianic, (*b*) non-Messianic, (*c*) double sense. 8: 1; 9: 7, Maher-shalal-hash-baz, deliverance from present and future judgments for those who fear God, of which Immanuel is the pledge, scene of his ministry, 9: 1, 2, its consequences, multiplication, joy, deliverance, end of war, vs. 3-5, person and titles, vs. 6, 7, Jewish, Rationalistic and Messianic interpretations. 9: 8; 10: 4, overthrow of Ephraim in four stanzas with like ending. 10: 5-34, overthrow of Assyria, Sennacherib's march, cut down as a forest. Chs. 11, 12, in contrast Messiah sprouts from root of Jesse, filled with the Spirit, restores Paradise, gathers the Gentiles and remnant of Israel, unites Judah and Ephraim, makes them victorious over all foes. Messianic passages: 7: 14-16; 9: 1-7. Chs. 11, 12, progressive climax.

(1) The prophets' thought was the security of the people. Their weapons are spiritual. The prophecy as given by Isaiah is fulfilled. The genuineness of ch. 12 has been questioned on insufficient grounds. Other prophets pass from prophecy to song and why not Isaiah? It has one of his characteristic passages in it.

(2) In time of Jothan, Isaiah was sent to a prosperous but carnal people. He was to startle them into obedience or vindicate God's righteousness. These being unheeded, he was to pass judgment on them and people would be swept away except the good.

(3) Support under affliction. 1st judgment has come and Assyria is rested on instead of God.

In early discourses ch. 1–6, pictured a prosperous people, but no prominence given to Messiah. In ch. 7–12, the Messiah is the source of aid. Each of these sections has a unity and completeness. The 1st six chs. advance regularly on each other till the glorious vision of the sixth. The 2, 7–12 follows the other.

(B) Chs. 13–27 ten burdens culminating in judgment on the whole world, followed by triumph of the Lord's people, two naturally corresponding series, twofold design, *masah*. (1.) chs. 13, 14 : 27, Babylon, the object of two burdens, here first connected with Judah's exile, to be overthrown by the Medes, 13 : 17, and become a perpetual desolation, vs. 19–22, in order to the deliverance of the chosen people, who sing their song of triumph over the oppressor's downfall, 14 : 1–23; Assyria's overthrow, vs. 24, 25. (2) 14 : 28–32, Philistia rejoicing in calamities of Judah, threatened with a formidable enemy from the north, by whom she shall be devastated in order to Zion's more complete establishment. (3.) chs. 15, 16, against Moab. (4.) chs. 17, 18, Damascus. (*a*) 17 : 1–11, denunciation of Syria, passing over, v. 3, into one against Ephraim its ally in assaulting Judah; (*b*) 17 : 12–14, denounces all succeeding invaders, hower numerous and powerful, with special reference to Sennacherib; (*c*) ch. 18, his fall announced to Ethiopia and other distant nations, who bring offerings to God. (5.) chs. 19, 20, Egypt; (*a*) 19 : 1–7, ruin under image of drying the Nile; (*b*) vs. 18–25, mercy, the salvation five times greater than the destruction, v. 18, altar, v. 19, union of Assyria and Egypt, 23, and of both with Israel, vs. 24, 26; (*c*) ch. 20, symbolical, action defining time of fulfillment. (6.) 21 : 1–10, Desert of the sea, *i. e.*, Babylon; Elam or Persia joined with the

Medes in its capture in a night of festivity. (7.) 21 : 11, 12, Dumah, silence, *i. e.*, Edom. (8.) 21 : 14-17 Arabia. (9.) ch. 22, valley of vision, *i. e.*, Jerusalem; (*a*) vs. 1-14, denunciation of the city; (*b*) vs. 15-19, degradation and exile of Shebna; (*c*) vs. 20-25, exaltation and establishment of Eliakim. (10.) ch. 23, Tyre to be overthrown by the Chaldeans, vs. 1-15, but to revive after seventy years, and her gain to be consecrated to the Lord, vs. 15-18. Ch. 24, General judgment of the whole world. Chs. 25-27, Judah's triumph and blessedness.

The first five and the last five burdens constitute two series. The first of each series are against Babylon, and the rest against nations subjugated by Assyria and Babylon, and by which the judgment was partially fulfilled. The second and third in each are against minor nations near Palestine. The third of each series is concluded with the time of its fulfillment, "in the years of an hireling," mean "years exactly measured." The object of the fourth of each series is the true covenant people. Damascus is equivalent to Israel here, because they are associated together. The fifth of each series is against prominent heathen powers, both of which series end with promises, and here, too, dates are given, but with reference to the duration and removal of judgments. Twofold design of these burdens: first, for the covenant people; second, for the nations themselves. All the nations named had been guilty of sins against the people of God, and it is so taught in the first six. Humiliation of Egypt is to remove objects (20 : 6) of idolatrous trust from covenant people. The design of announcement to the Gentiles, is, first, that the judgment of one (18 : 7) might lead others to trust in God; and secondly, the nations themselves are to be converted to God, *e. g.*, Egypt and Tyre; Assyria is mentioned with Egypt, same purpose toward all. These individual judgments are given as parts of God's general judgment of the world, shown both by the beginnings and ends of the burdens. Thus, 13 : 6-13, mentions convulsions of nature which did not happen in the overthrow of Babylon, but they are put here because it is viewed as one scene in God's providential work of judgment, as in Matt. 24: 29; and in 14 : 26, the character of the judgment is stated, " upon the whole earth;" and in the 24th ch., the judgments terminate upon the world at large. These judgments have same title affixed to each, viz.: " burden." This word explained, 1, derived from *nasa*—" to lift up the voice." Therefore it means solemn utterance, a prophecy irrespective of the character of its contents. 2. From same root in sense of "to lift up and carry," hence "a burden," *i. e.*, a prohecy of threatening import. Proof, *a.* universal usage of word, being used with prophecies of grievous character. *b.* agrees better with radical meaning of verb, and with the ordinary meaning of noun. 3. Agrees better with syntax, the noun stands, in construct, before name of that which is object of prophecy, *e. g.*, burden of Babylon—load which B. is to bear. The utterance of Babylon would not convey the idea of the syntax. The fact that these were genuine prophecy is strengthened by the use of such enigmatical title, which would not have been used by a forger. In the first six chapters exile of Judah is predicted, but hitherto the agent has not been named, but now Assyria, though only a province, is here declared to be the agent, hence it is the subject of two distinct burdens. In the 13th ch. Babylon is to be overthrown by the Medes, and this in 14 : 1, 2, is declared to be for the deliverance of the covenant people. Hence he reverts to the nearest foe, by whom the first blow is to be struck. Ch. 14 : 24, 25, repeats Syria's overthrow for the comfort of the people. The second burden has a title in 14 : 28, denunciation against Palestine in the year Ahaz died, and they are threatened with destruction from the north. In the fourth burden, which begins against Assyria, and then proceeds to prophesy against Ephraim, since it and Syria were to be devastated by Assyria. Then he passes to the most distant powers under the name of Ethiopia, who are exhorted to behold how God would destroy all his enemies. The fifth is against Egypt. Five cities of Egypt are to embrace the true religion, to one that is to be destroyed, and an altar is to be erected to the Lord, which may mean that Jerusalem shall no longer be the only place of sacrifice. If signifying altar of witness, it simply implies conversion of Egypt. Sixth burden vs. Desert of the Sea. This Babylon v. 9. Sea—Euphrates. This term sometimes applied to large rivers, especially such as overflow their banks. Desert is a reference to what it is to become. This second judgment vs. Babylon goes beyond previous one since 1. Persia is added to Media as an instrument. 2. The capture is predicted as happening on a night of festivity. Seventh burden vs. Dennah. Evidently means Edom, from resemblance to name Idumea. It has reference to condition to which it will come, *i. e.*, silence and destruction. Eighth burden vs. Ara-

bia. Ninth burden vs. the valley of vision—Jerusalem where visions and prophecies were given. Thus both branches of Israel are included in these judgments, ten tribes in first under Damascus: Judah in second under valley of vision. Reason for judgment vs. Jerusalem is her association with Edom. This is followed by prediction concerning two individuals, *a.* 15-19 Shebna, whose degradation and exile is foretold as leader and example of the sinning people. *b.* 20-25 Eliakim, whose exaltation and establishment is foretold as type of faithful remnant. Tenth burden vs. Tyre, stating time of her remaining under judgment, with promise of restoration. Ch. 24, general judgment on whole world, resulting in triumph of God's people and manifestation of his glory. Chs. 25-27. Judah's triumph and God's glory, an advance.

(*C*) Chs. 28-35. As the time for the Assyrian invasion came on, the warnings and the comforts needed to be repeated. Ch. 28: 1-6, gives the overthrow of kingdom of ten tribes, followed in rest of section by rebukes and threatenings of Judah, with interjected promises of Assyria's overthrow and Judah's deliverance. This section begins with woe. 28: 1 is first date and Samaria is still standing. The first woe is against Samaria, a proud city, drunken. In that day "the Lord of Hosts shall he for a crown of glory." 4: 2 the parallel passage supplies key for 28: 1. The branch of Jehovah is not then prosperity of an abundant harvest. Where priests and prophets are so associated that they err, they are swallowed up. Isaiah tells them they can have what they want, but God will speak to them in strange tongues, in precept upon precept, line upon line. Foreign invasion shall issue in your destruction.

They claimed to have made an understanding with death so that they would not be harmed—meaning that they had made an alliance with Egypt. They have broken alliance with Assyria and gone to Egypt against all their vows. The Lord says, I have a "foundation," seeing that those who trusted God need not hasten to leave this foundation. Judgment is his. They were exposing themselves to his righteous judgment. Your alliance with Egypt will not save you for Assyria will overcome. This frightful scourge which Assyria brings will be the word of God to you. You are too long for your bed. Be ye not scoffers. The cornerstone is rightly applied to Jews by Peter and Paul. The section closed appropriately in ch. 28. Everything is done in order.

Ploughman don't plough for sake of ploughing. He sows later and all preparatory work is for sake of the grain. When grain is ripe and gathered, it is not threshed indiscriminately. He is not threshing for sake of threshing, but he afterwards grinds it for bread. So Jehovah has an end in view, and maybe the treatment may be severe, but it must be for the good of the people.

Isaiah listened to as if it was nothing, but they worked in silence, so that Isaiah would not see them and give God's will against them. This pretending to' honor God, and yet not doing it, is to call forth a marvelous work:—woe to them concealing their plans from the Lord. He tells them that in a short time there will be great changes. The meek and poor would rejoice in the Lord after the wise men should perish. After overthrow they would recognize God. We have traced their hidden scheme to trust Egypt through two stages.

(D) Chs. 36, 37. This section is wound up by these two chapters which give the fact of the invasion by Assyria. Isaiah's prophecy at the time, and the miraculous deliverance.

3. (A) Chs. 38, 39, are introductory. They give the prophet's ministry. After such a judgment, and such a deliverance, it might be hoped that the people would turn to the Lord. But it is not so. A better prince than Ahaz is now on the throne, and yet Hezekiah had not escaped the taint of former kings. His heart was lifted up with pride, and to the messengers sent to him by the king of Babylon with messages of congratulation that he had recovered, he shows the treasures of the Lord's house. This display of the treasures served to excite the cupidity of the king, and caused him to take them away from Judah. The people are not allowed to gloat over the defeat of Sennacherib. As far as this was allowed, it was committed to Nahum. Isaiah announces the Babylonish captivity. From this time he devotes himself to the work of comfort; not here and there a ray of comfort, as in the preceding part of the prophecy, but in the great body of what follows. The captivity was so dreadful that some great thing was needed to prevent the true people of God from falling into utter despair. So Isaiah, a prophet of a former age, prepared the way for them. It is for a like reason that Daniel was sent to tell the times of Antiochus Epiphanes, which were to come long after. Isaiah tells of God's great purpose respecting his people. He shows the occasion, design and issue of their suffering.

Their sufferings (*a*) arose not from God's weakness but their sins, (*b*) were designed to fit them for and further the accomplishment of their task, (*c*) would issue in the blessedness and glory. These topics are intermingled in the chapter.

(*B*) Chs. 40–66. Each division, of nine chapters each, is distinguished, sometimes by a particular event, without being exclusively occupied by it. Babylon and Cyrus are nowhere else named. This election is divided into—

(1.) Chs. 40–48, Deliverance from exile, characteristic chap. 45. (2.) Chs. 49–57, Sufferings and triumph of Messiah, ch. 53. (3.) Chs. 58–66, Future glory of God's people, ch. 60. Shadowed forth, 40 : 2. Mission of Covenant People, includes work of Messiah, both embraced under name Servant of the Lord; (*a*) appropriateness of title; (*b*) analogies to seed of Abraham, the prophet, son of David, Christ and His church in N. T.; (*c*) N. T.—Acts 13 : 47, comp. Isa. 49 : 6; 2 Cor. 6 : 2; comp. Isa. 49 : 8; also Jer. 11 : 19; comp. Isa. 53 : 7; (*d*) applicability to all the passages. Can not mean Israel to the exclusion of Messiah; (*a*) called Israel 49 : 3, but distinguished from them, 42 : 6; 49 : 5, 6, as their mediator and restorer; (*b*) his atoning death, ch. 53. Nor Isaiah or the prophets: (*a*) Mission not to Gentiles, (*b*) nor sufferings vicarious. Nor Cyrus. Nor even Messiah exclusively, for he is charged (42 : 9) with unfaithfulness and sin.

1. Chs. 40–48. Ch. 40, Omnipotence of Him who offers deliverance, voice crying in wilderness, v. 3. Ch. 41, contrasted impotence of idols; they can do nothing, but God will raise up Cyrus and redeem His people. Ch. 42, destiny of God's servant, which neither God's seeming apathy, nor his own character and condition shall obstruct. Chs. 43, 44, God will certainly befriend His people in spite of idols and diviners. Chs. 45–47, Cyrus predicted by name, the humiliation of Babylon and the deliverance of God's captive people.

2. Chs. 49–57. Ch. 49, Servant of Lord complains of want of success; he shall accomplish the salvation, not of Israel only, but of the ends of the earth. The blessedness thence resulting, 49 : 12; 66 : 8, confirmed by former benefits, viz.: Multiplication of Abraham's seed, 51 : 2, deliverance from Egypt, v. 9, and from Assyria, 52 : 4, and twice interrupted by the sufferings of the Servant of the Lord, 50 : 6, and ch. 53. Blessings flowing from this vicarious death, ch. 54, offered freely to all without restriction, ch. 55, expressly extended to sons of strangers and those ceremonially

debarred from covenant privileges, 56 : 1–8 ; the heavy doom of apostates and sinners, 56 : 9 ; 57 : 21.

3. Chs. 58–66. The wickedness and hypocrisy of the people the cause of their suffering, chs. 58, 59, and call for divine intervention, 59 : 16, both for mercy and vengeance, bringing salvation to Zion, chs. 60–62, and judgment on Edom, the type of her foes, 63 : 1–6. The Servant of the Lord for the last time, 61 : 1–3; comp. Luke 4 : 18, 19. The prophet's prayer for the speedy accomplishment of these things 63 : 7 ; 64 : 12. The Lord's answer, chs. 65, 66, the wicked shall be cut off. God's true servants preserved and blessed, new heavens and new earth, paradise restored, God's people brought back, Gentiles made priests, all flesh worship. Extension of salvation to Gentile fore-shadowed in call of Abraham, Gen. 12 : 3, recognized in Mosaic period, Num. 14 : 21, and by Psalmist, 22 : 27, 28 ; 72 : 8, etc., and taught with great fullness by Isaiah ; this was the design of (*a*) the appointment of the Servant of the Lord, 42 : 1–4, 6 ; (*b*) the exaltation to be bestowed on Israel, 2 : 2–4 ; 60 : 3 ; (*c*) the judgments on the heathen, whether (*a*) the overthrow of an empire aspiring to be universal, 10 : 34 ; 11 : 9 ; (*b*) the punishment of individual nations resulting in the conversion of others, 18 : 7, or their own, chs. 19–23, or, (*c*) the judgment on all nations, 24 : 14, 15 ; 59 : 18, 19. Represented as (*a*) a subjugation, 11 : 14 ; (*b*) voluntary accession, 2 : 3 ; 11 : 10 ; (*c*) rendering service, 14 : 1, 2 ; 49 : 22, 23, (*d*) union on an equal footing, 19 : 24 ; 56 : 6, 8 ; 66 : 21, (*e*) substitution in place of the rejected sinners of Israel, 65 : 1, 2. Expressed mostly in O. T. forms ; coming up to Zion, offering sacrifices, etc., yet occasional intimations of their temporary character, (*a*) physical impossibility literally understood, 66 : 23 ; (*b*) unessential nature of outward forms, 1 : 11–15 ; 58 : 2–7 ; (*c*) removal of Levitical restrictions, 19 : 19 ; 64 : 4, 5.

GENUINENESS OF ISAIAH.

External evidence is almost perfect for Isaiah's genuineness. Josephus says, that Cyrus moved to liberate Israelites from reading prophecy of Isaiah regarding himself. Isaiah named in N. T. 22 times. Authorship of these last chapters was never doubted till lately.

For correspondence of Isaiah, 2 : 2–4, and Micah, 4 : 1–3. (*Vide* Alexander's Commentary.) Also of the four histori-

cal chapters, 36-39, and 2 Kings 18: 13; 20: 19. The burden of Moab, chs. 15 and 16 (see 16: 13, 14,) in consequence of its closing verses has been thought to be the production of a prophet older than Isaiah, and simply re-affirmed by him. It is more probable that Isaiah here repeated an earlier prophecy of his own. This prophecy is not in form, but substantially what has been predicted by prophets before him. The question of genuineness is very different from this. Every prophecy from the beginning to the close of the book which implies a foresight of the Babylonish exile, is said to be spurious on the ground that such foresight is contrary to nature *e. g.*, two burdens of Babylon, 13 and 14 chs., 21: 1-10, and the comfort (40-66 chs.) given to the people of God.

Reply.—**1.** Skeptics from a disbelief of prophetic foresight have no influence with those who are Christians. It is simply a begging of the question.

2. Objectors have not a pretext on any external ground. The entire book claims to be the book of Isaiah. So asserted in 2 Chron. 32: 32. Alluded to in Ecclesiasticus 48: 22-25. Of the 21 times in which Isaiah is mentioned in the N. T., 11 are from this section. No MSS. or versions leave them out. The book has been in Jewish custody from the earliest times, and no doubt has been expressed until recent times. They must have guarded it carefully.

3 The allegations that these sections differ in style from the other parts of the book have been made in subserviency to the objections already named. There was no discovery of difference in style for 24 centuries, and it was first brought forward when the book was given up on other grounds. What one critic condemns as inelegant, another lauds to the skies. They are quite at variance as to whether these sections differ from one another. They all agree that they differ from Isaiah's style in other places. When they undertake to point to specific differences in style, they bring up such words and phrases as do not occur in other parts of the book. This may be true if it be allowed that nothing is to be accepted which is found in one book of a writer, but not in another. As far as there is any difference of style in Isaiah, it may be accounted for by the difference of subject and occasion, or difference of purpose, if it be admitted that the last seven chapters had a different purpose. These differences of style are the variations of style of a writer of great genius. The changes are due partly to advancing years. The objection of the existence of words and phrases which indicate a later time than that of Isaiah, is established by most uncertain data. Supposititious senses are laid to them. Words which occur in no other writings of that time are said to belong to another period. Sometimes words are found to agree with prophets of an earlier period, and these are rejected.

4. It is impossible to account for the prophecies in question being found in the canon if they were not his own. They were either put there innocently, or by fraud, but how a writer in the time of the exile could succeed in passing one of his writing for those of Isaiah, which were at the time of the formation of the canon is unimaginable, and the greater the number of writers the greater the complexity. How these chapters could have been innocently put into the canon, it is impossible to see. How writings could have appeared in the time of Isaiah, and been mistaken for his is inconceivable. This difficulty is greatly exaggerated by the number of spurious passages. If these passages were taken away the symmetry of the book would be exceedingly marred. It is objected to the two burdens of Babylon, chs. 13, 14, 21: 1-10, that the exile is not predicted, but implied, therefore the writer must have lived in the midst of the exile. *Answer.*—The prophets often speak of future events as if they were present, their certainty is so great. The exile had been already foretold by Isaiah, chap. 5. It had been foretold by Moses in Lev. 26. Isaiah in ch. 39 declares who the agents of this calamity were to be. He speaks of the birth, death and sufferings of the Messiah as past. Are we, therefore, to conclude that these portions were written after the death of Christ?

Positive Proofs of Genuineness.—(1.) The title of the first of these burdens (13: 1) expressly alludes to Isaiah. It was put there by the prophet himself, for (*a*) the title was necessary to the understanding of the prophecy. (*b*) From analogy of other burdens. (*c*) Such enigmatical titles would not likely have come from a forger. (2.) 14: 24-27, The concluding part of this burden is admitted to belong to Isaiah. Critics have in vain attempted to find a place for this passage in other portions of the prophecy. It refers to Assyria, but where is there mention of Assyria at the time of the exile, when Assyria had passed away long before? (3.) 21: 1-6, By the general structure of the burdens, and from the enigmatical title, introducing the figure of the watchman. The structure of these burdens is like all the

others, therefore they were written by Isaiah. (4.) The prophetic foresight will not be obviated by transferring him to the latest period possible—exile. Even when Cyrus was before the walls of Babylon, no one would believe he could overcome the city.

Objections to 40-66.—(**I.**) The people are represented as already in exile, but (*a*) this is possible far less frequently than is alleged. Those passages which refer to the exile or return are few, and many which are said to relate to it, refer to some other result; *e. g*, " highway " refers to God's preparation for conversion of the Gentiles; "release of prisoner" —release from trouble, " pools of water "—joyful changes of any kind, and when return from exile is promised it is a return from all quarters, not merely from Babylon, (*b*) this objection is inconsistent with the fact that the prophet urges his prediction of coming events in proof of God's foreknowledge and superiority over idols. 41 : 22-27: 43 : 9-12; 45 : 3; 46 : 9-11. (*c*) These passages show a better state of things existing before the exile. The temple was still standing, 66 : 6-20; 58 : 2-6; 43 : 24; 65 : 11. Idolatry was still existing, 66 : 17; 65 : 11; and in such forms as more probably derived from Egypt than from Babylon. The people are courting alliance with foreign monarchs; their judgment is represented as future. The critics explain this by assuming the record of these facts to be an earlier fragment. But this is begging the question. (*d*) The force of the objection is derived from confounding the ideal with the actual present. Such is the assurance of the prophet that he regards these events as actually present. That these events were regarded by the prophet as really future is seen from the fact; (1) that the terms are too broad to be confined to exile; (2) that some other deliverance than return from Babylonish exile is referred to. For the evil from which the deliverance foreshadowed and the glory which followed it are different; (3) specific reference to Babylon and the exile are singularly few, but this could hardly be the case if the writer was writing during the exile. Admitted that the specific predictions with reference to Cyrus are remarkable, yet they are few and the whole description is general. If they were uttered before the event, there is prevision whether Isaiah wrote them or not; (4) the writer transports himself to various points of time; *e. g*., exile, fall of Babylon, time of Messiah, time of Israel's glory. But confessed not written after the latest point. Therefore prevision is involved.

(**2.**) The predictions are plain till close of the exile, but vague thereafter, which shows the standpoint of the writer. But (1) though the prediction of the fact of the exile and its end are sufficiently clear to be proof of the divine foreknowledge, yet the expressions are mostly general. While on the other hand, what is predicted of Christ and his work is more specific than the definite predictions referring to the exile. (2) This apparent change of style is to be accounted for by the fact that prophecy is the disclosure of just so much of the future as will furnish useful lessons. But in this latter part of the ministry of the prophet, the thing most neces sary was to prepare the people for the next event of God's judgment, viz: their actual overthrow by Babylon and ultimate glory of Israel. So the language with reference to this event needs to be plain; (3) in so far as the fact alleged is true, it rather makes against the critic. For it would be naturally inferred from the statements of Cyrus and return being followed immediately by Messianic predictions, that Messianic period was to come at once. But if these predictions were written after these events such an idea would have been impossible, for the poor realization of any glory in the return would give the idea that Messianic period was not at hand. But if written before these events it involves prevision. If, however, written by Isaiah as supernatural predictions the juxtaposition is accounted for, because in all his prophecies Messiah is the background. (4.) Josephus, (Ant. XI. 1, 2,) says that these predictions were shown to Cyrus and were among the things that induced him to rescue the people of God, which would account for his restoration of them. This corroborated Ezra 1 : 2. (5.) The argument from expressions peculiar to this section is balanced by the fact that there are expressions here, which are found in acknowledged parts of the book, *e. g.*, Holy One of Israel, 12 times in previous parts; 14 times here.

3. The theme is one which could have had no interest to Isaiah or his contemporaries. He speaks of evils which then had no existence, whereas the people wanted release from present evils of Syria and Assyria. But (1) we hold that this is a question that is to be decided only by a survey of his writings, with relation to the times in which he lived and wrote. Now, at the opening of his ministry, which was in the prosperous times of Josiah, he declares future judgments which he afterwards unfolds. When the first blow (Syria) came, he declared its failure and yet announced a far more

THE BOOK OF ~~MOSES~~ Isaiah.

BY PROFESSOR W. H. GREEN, LL.D., OF PRINCETON THEOLOGICAL SEMINARY.

V.

THE UNITY OF ISAIAH.

After the Book of Isaiah had passed as the genuine production of the prophet for twenty-five hundred years unchallenged and unsuspected, the critics profess to have discovered within the last century that it contains two distinct series of prophecies, diverse in occasion, character, and style, and proceeding from different authors who lived a century and a half apart. The one series, amounting to not quite half of the book, is confessed to be beyond question the work of the prophet to whom the whole has heretofore been uniformly ascribed. The other series embraces every prophecy, from the beginning of the book to its close, which implies or has been thought to imply a foresight of the Babylonish exile. The suspected passages are accordingly the two burdens of Babylon (xiii, 1-xiv, 23, and xxi, 1-10), the denunciation and triumph (chapters xxiv-xxvii, and xxxiv, xxxv), and the comfort to the people in prospect of the exile (chapters xl-lxvi). Some hesitating voices have also declared against the burden of Egypt (chapter xix), on the assumption that it describes a state of things subsequent to the time of Isaiah; others withdraw all objection on the ground that it can be brought within the life of Isaiah by referring it to an Assyrian invasion. Some cast away the burden upon Tyre (chapter xxiii), because of the mention of the Chaldeans (verse 13); others save the chapter by ejecting that troublesome word, or by supposing that the Chaldeans are here spoken of, not as an independent power, but as subjugated by the

Assyrians. According to Dr. Driver (*Literature of the Old Testament*, page 205), xxi, 1-10, is by Isaiah if it refers to "a siege of Babylon by the Assyrians in Isaiah's own time;" but if it refers to "the conquest of Babylon by Cyrus," it is to be ascribed "to a prophet living toward the close of the exile."

This vacillation of the critics shows that the one conclusive consideration with them is that no passage can be admitted to be genuine if this implies the admission of superhuman foresight. All other arguments are subordinate to this. Arguments which are held to prove a passage spurious by such critics as think it to imply a supernatural knowledge of the future, are set aside as insufficient by those who fancy that they can so explain it as to avoid this implication. And the same critic will attach no importance to arguments of spuriousness in one passage which he urges as convincing in another, if in the former passage this expedient is not necessary to escape the evidence of supernatural foresight, and in the latter it is.

It is not pretended that there is any external proof of the late date of these disputed chapters. So far as we have any means of tracing the Book of Isaiah, they would seem to have been always included in it. All existing manuscripts and all ancient versions exhibit the Book of Isaiah without variation precisely as we now have it, the disputed portions as well as the rest. Ancient authorities referring to the book make no discrimination, and manifestly accept the whole as equally undoubted. There is explicit testimony to Isaiah's authorship in Isa. i, 1, which is the title of the whole book, and a special testimony in regard to chapters xiii and xiv in xiii, 1. The author or compiler of Kings, in adopting Isa. xxxvi-xxxix into his book, gives his confirmation to the fact that Isaiah predicted the Babylonish exile (2 Kings xx, 16-18). "The vision of Isaiah the prophet, the son of Amoz," is referred to, as well known, in 2 Chron. xxxii, 32. It is distinctly alluded to in Eccles. xlviii, 22-25, where special reference is made to the disputed chapters. The language of the decree of Cyrus (Ezra i, 2) contains an evident allusion to Isa. xliv, 28; xlv, 13. And Josephus (*Antiquities*, xi, 1, 2) says that Cyrus was moved to restore the Jews to their own land and to aid in rebuilding their temple by reading these prophecies of Isaiah respecting himself. When the Greek Septuagint Version was made the Book of Isaiah contained precisely what it does now. Isaiah is spoken of by name twenty-two times in the New Testament, in eleven of which he is connected with citations from chapters xl-lxvi.

The denial of Isaiah's authorship of the prophecies in question rests upon the three following propositions, namely:

1. The theme of these prophecies is one that could have been of no interest to Isaiah or to his contemporaries. They promise deliverance from evils which then had no existence, and from foes which were not the real foes that the people had then to dread. They craved present relief from Assyrian oppressions and invasions, not restoration from a Babylonish exile which had not yet taken place, and of which there was no immediate prospect.

2. This exile is not predicted, but assumed as then actually existing. All the expressions employed re-

formidable blow from Assyria, which, however, would not be successful. As neither of these was to accomplish this judgment, it was natural that he should show by whom it was to be accomplished, which he does by declaring the overthrow of Babylon. Yet this is not to be complete. Thus we see (*a*) that in these acknowledged portions of the book the prophet speaks of a distant evil, when another one was present before the people. Therefore a similar method cannot be made an argument against the genuineness of this section. (*b*) That all these predictions of judgments and ultimate deliverances, are but development of one theme, and since same ideas of deliverance and judgment are present in this section, the presumption is that it is the following out of the same theme. (2.) On the contrary, it was a theme of intense interest to Israel, since it concerned their national existence and the accomplishment of God's promise.

4. The theme has reference to an event too remote to have affected Israel. (Captivity.) But (1.) This is assuming that the critic has the right to determine the time over which prophecy is to range. (2.) Messianic prophecies of the book relate to an event much further removed than this. (3.) On the hypothesis that these are the real declarations of God, the propriety of their relating to a far distant event is seen. (4.) We must remember that, while, from the development of history, this event appears far removed from the time of the prophet, yet its date was not known to prophet or people at that time. As far as they knew the judgment was imminent. (5.) This argument shows the inconsistency of the theory, and since the very absence of remoteness is urged by them against the inspiration of the book.

PREDICTIONS OF OLD TESTAMENT AS TO SUFFERINGS OF THE MESSIAH.

They are not first revealed to Isaiah, but are really made known from the first promise in the garden. Then they are brought out in those Psalms which refer to the righteous sufferer. They reach their fullest development in Isaiah. Lowly origin; despised of men; obstacles to his work; personal violence. After Isaiah they are taken up by Daniel. Cut off for the people (9: 24–26.) Then by Zechariah. Lowly (9: 9); an object of aversion (11: 8); sold for silver (11: 13); smitten by a sword (13: 7). Isaiah combines the various methods of all the O. T. prophets. He shows results viewed (*a*) from the appointment of Israel and M. as servant of Jehovah; (*b*) as judgments on the heathen. Either judgments on individual nations, which would bring the rest to acknowledge God, or judgments on all, which would bring them all to God.

He shows the relations of the Gentiles to the Jews subjugation (11: 14), voluntary accession (60: 3), a rendering of service (14: 2), union on a level (56: 6, 8), substitution in place of Israel (65: 1, 2). Their coming is mostly described under the forms of the ancient ritual, while its spiritual character is shown by coupling it with physical impossibilities.

NAHUM.

Name.—"A comfort." Called "the Elkoshite." Probably not a patronymic, but a local designation—the place where he was born or lived. But Elkosh is nowhere mentioned in the Bible. Jerome and Eusebius,—a small village in Galilee. Some—same as Capernaum (village of Nahum). Both are mere conjectures.

Date.—Nowhere distinctly stated. 1. From its position among minor prophets it might be assigned any place between reigns of Hezekiah and Josiah. 2. The inferences made rest really upon the interpretation of 1: 9–14. Some say this refers to the Captivity of Manasseh by king of Assyria, and infer that it was the last invasion by Assyria. But (*a*) it merely means that when God shall judge their oppressors they shall be overthrown, not necessarily that they shall never come again (*b*) It is scarcely probable that the prophet speaking in time of Manasseh, would merely refer to the coming deliverance without allusion to the kings. (*c*) According to this hypothesis he would be the only prophet in the reign of Manasseh, which reign, with that of Amos, is regarded as without prophecy, merely separating between the Assyrian and Chaldean Periods.

A better interpretation refers the passage to the invasion of Sennacherib in the reign of Hezekiah. Proof:—(*a*) The bonds that are to be broken are not those of an individual (Manasseh) but of Judah, the people. (*b*) The circumstances of that invasion seem to be specially referred to. *e. g.* Evil counsel of Rabshekah v. 11. Sudden overthrow of Assyrians. v. 12. Murder of Sennacherib. Then the only

garding it imply, not that it was anticipated in the distant future, but that it was the veritable present. The time and circumstances of the writer, as inferred from his production, are not those of Isaiah, but of the later years of the Babylonish exile.

3. The style and diction of these chapters are wholly unlike those of the chapters which are admitted to be Isaiah's.

In opposition to which we maintain:

1. The theme of these prophecies is such as might be expected from Isaiah, and forms a proper complement to his other revelations.

2. The revelation here made is in analogy with his other disclosures of the future, and those of other prophets, and is such as could not have been written during or after the events referred to. It bears internal evidence of being a prophetic and not an historical survey of those events.

3. The style and diction offer no obstruction to their being regarded as the genuine productions of Isaiah.

I. The question whether the theme of the disputed prophecies is an appropriate one for Isaiah is not to be decided magisterially or capriciously, but after a careful survey of his writings in their relation to the times in which he lived. Early in his ministry he predicts the utter desolation of the land (vi, 11-13) by foreign foes (v, 26-30). When the first wave of calamity broke over Judah in the reign of Ahaz he declared to the terrified king and people that the invasion by Syria and Ephraim would be unsuccessful and would soon be over (vii, 4-7), and that Assyria, which would press Judah more sorely still, would likewise fail (viii, 9, 10). It is precisely in the line of these revelations that he should make known what power it was which was destined to accomplish the predicted desolation. As he had alleviated the fears respecting Syria by pointing out that it was not Syria in the present so much as Assyria in the future that was to be dreaded, so in prospect of the evils to be wrought by Assyria he diverts attention from them to the incomparably greater disaster to be wrought by Babylon. As he gave assurance of the defeat of Syria by declaring the downfall of its more formidable successor (viii, 7-10; x, 5-34), so he builds a fresh argument of the overthrow of Assyria (xiv, 24-27) by exhibiting (chapters xiii, xiv) the certainty and completeness of the downfall of Babylon, which was to arise upon its ruins. As he chastised the dependence of Ahaz upon Assyria by declaring that Assyria would be a direr source of evil than that from which he was then seeking relief, so in like manner he chastises Hezekiah's vain display to the messengers of the King of Babylon (chapter xxxix) by announcing that it was from this very Babylon that Judah's overthrow should come. And as Isaiah's previous predictions of foreign oppression are uniformly followed by promises of the ultimate deliverance and triumph of Israel and the downfall of their foes (ix, 1-7; xi, xii), so in the case of Babylon and every other oppressor (chapters xiv, xxiv-xxvii, xxxiv, xxxv, xl-lxvi).

When now in the book ascribed to Isaiah we find this series of prophecies relating to Babylon intermingled with and attached to the other series relating to Assyria, and discover that both alike are but the more explicit unfolding of what was already involved in his initial predictions (chapters i-vi), and that they are in all respects parallel the one to the other, that they are based on the same principles, inculcate the same lessons, and are developed in the same identical manner, by what right can it be affirmed that the one theme is appropriate to Isaiah and that the prophecies which treat of it are undoubtedly his; but that the other series of prophecies must be denied to be his because the theme, which is in its essence identical with the preceding, is one which Isaiah could not have treated because it lacked interest for him and his contemporaries?

But it is claimed that the event contemplated was too remote to have affected either prophet or people in Isaiah's days. Cyrus and the fall of Babylon and the return from captivity were a century and a half away. Who then is to define the limit of time over which prophecy may range? Isaiah's predictions of Messiah, whether in his humiliation or in his kingdom and glory, look to a period still more remote. And although a long interval did, in fact, elapse before the Babylonish exile and the restoration from it, the existence of such an interval and the length of it were not revealed. For aught that the people or the prophet knew, these were imminent, and might take place at any time after the respite of fifteen years promised to Hezekiah (xxxviii, 5; xxxix, 8). So far is the prophecy from indicating the remoteness of the events in question, even in the view of the objectors to its genuineness, that the absence of any such indication is their chief argument against it, the force of which we shall presently examine. When and how all had its historical fulfillment is a very proper question, if the matter under investigation were the divine origin and inspiration of the prophecy. But whether it was ever fulfilled at all, and if so, when, is quite irrelevant now, when the question before us is solely that of Isaiah's authorship. If these predictions had turned out to be vague, unfounded anticipations, to which no future had ever corresponded, the present objectors would have found little difficulty in admitting them to have been from Isaiah. If the subject be approached with no prepossessions as to the nature of prophecy, and none either for or against the possibility or reality of supernatural inspiration, the theme of the disputed prophecies can create no surprise. It is in strict analogy with his acknowledged prophecies, and is their appropriate sequel. The fact that they were fulfilled long after, with an accuracy and a minuteness which show them to have been inspired of God, can surely not be urged by any candid man as a reason for discrediting them.

Moreover, when his contemporary, Micah, explicitly predicts the desolation of Jerusalem, the Babylonish captivity, and deliverance from it, with what propriety can it be affirmed that these topics are unsuitable in Isaiah? Micah sought to startle his auditors out of their presumptuous confidence by declaring to them (iii. 12): "Zion shall for your sake be plowed as a field, and Jerusalem shall become heaps, and the mountain of the house as the high places of a forest." And to the people personified as "the daughter of Zion" he announces (iv, 10), "Thou shalt go forth out of the city, and shalt dwell in the field, and shalt come even unto Babylon; there shalt thou be rescued; there shall the Lord redeem thee from the hand of

question remains as to whether it was before or after the first invasion. If after, then the preterites are historical; if before, they are prophetical.

Inferences have also been drawn from the mention of the capture of No-Ammon, (Thebes) 3: 8–10. But the date is uncertain.

Structure.—Double title. 1: 1. Subject, the burden of Nineveh: author—the book of the vision of Nahum, the Elkoshite. Contents divided into 3 parts. (*a*) Ch. 1. God coming to judgment: the object being Nineveh. (*b*) ch. 2. Overthrow of Nineveh is exhibited to the prophet. Preliminary of the siege, v. 2, 3. Assault, 4, 5. Ineffectual defence, 6–8. Sack, 9. Resulting desolation, 10–12. Pledge of Jehovah for its fullment, 13. (*c*) Ch. 3. Repetition of the same subject in which the act is justified by giving reasons for it in form of charges against the city. Crime and fraud, v. 1–3. Whoredoms and witchcrafts, 4–7. *i. e.*, the political and commercial management by which Nineveh reduced nations to ruin. Fate of No-Ammon is told as typical of Nineveh's downfall. This was fulfilled in the taking of Nineveh by Cyaxeres and Nabo-Polassar, 606 B. C. From that date the city began to decline. The instrument is not named, only described. The special mention of cavalry corresponds to Media.

CHALDEAN PERIOD.

Separated from preceding period by the ungodly reigns of Manasseh, 55 yrs., Amon 2 yrs., and the people under them were very bad. Manasseh was worse than any king Israel ever had. He erected altars of idolatry, even in the temple, and he filled Jerusalem with innocent blood, 2 Kings 21: 1–16; 2 Chron. 33: 1–9. Manasseh repented and reformed at the close of his reign, but with so little effect upon the popular corruption that the author of Kings passes it over in silence.

Such was the state of things when Josiah, at 8 years of age, came to the throne. At 12 years of age, he began to purge the land of idolatry. At 18 years he repaired God's house, and abolished idolatry. After 31 years of reign he was slain at Megiddo. Four kings followed, and all were wicked. Of these, the first and last were sons of Josiah by different mothers. Jehoahaz, 3 mos., was carried to Egypt, and died there. Jehoiakim, 11 yrs.; he was placed over the kingdom by the king of Egypt; he exceeded the others in wickedness. In the fourth year, Nebuchadnezzar completed his preparation, and captured Jerusalem, Jer. 46: 2. The first deportation of exiles was at this time, and the 70 yrs. captivity must be reckoned from this time. The city still continued for some years. The rebellion of Jehoiakin (3 mos.) called for a new demonstration on the part of Nebuchadnezzar. Zedekiah was a weak prince, in fear of the nobles of the land. He did not protect Jeremiah, or obey his message. His reign of 11 yrs. terminated with the destruction of the city.

Observation.—1. This period is distinguished from the preceding by the greatly increased and increasing corruption. Several signs of this: (*a*) The character of the kings was an influential cause of the state of things. In the former period Ahaz is the only wicked king; in this, Josiah is the only good one. And even in his time the idolatry and corruption were only put down for a time. When this was past they became worse than ever. (*b*) Obduracy in the face of judgment. In the former period, on the approach of the Assyrians, Hezekiah went in sackcloth, and in prayer to God. But now Jehudi (Jer. 36: 23, 24) cut in pieces the roll of Jeremiah, and threw it into the fire. Zedekiah refused to obey the prophets, though the enemy was before the city, Jeremiah, chs. 37, 38. And the people were confirmed in evil, Jer. 44: 17, 18. (*c*) Persecution and martyrdom of the prophets of God. The former prophets complained that the people had not obeyed their messages, but there was no violence done them. Even judgments of which they were forewarned were defied, Is. 5: 19; Amos 5: 18; 7: 12, 13. Now they are the subjects of every form of abuse, 2 Chron. 36: 16; Jer. 26: 20-23. (*d*) Prevalence and influence of false prophets. The existence of false prophets was intimated in the previous period, but now they appear with an influence and a power such as they never had before. By their promises they break the force of the messages of the true prophets, Jer. 28. This is an index of corruption, especially of the noble classes. (*e*) Presumptuous trust in covenant privileges, even while disregarding the conditions of promise, Jer. 7: 4. Even the captivity of the ten tribes instead of confirming to them the threats and warnings of the true prophets, bolstered their conceit, because the fact of their preservation thus far proved God's special favor. And Jo-

thine enemies." These predictions are not only attributed to Micah in the book which bears his name, but his utterance of the former has besides the attestation of Jer. xxvi, 18. And this is the more significant in its bearing on the subject now before us, as there is in many respects an intimate relation between the Books of Micah and Isaiah. Isaiah borrowed the theme of his discourse (chapters ii-iv) from Micah iv, 1-3, which immediately follows the prediction of the desolation of Jerusalem and the temple. And it is not surprising that he should elsewhere dwell upon that great catastrophe which Micah so unambiguously announces.

II. It is argued that these prophecies belong to the period, not of Isaiah, but of the exile, because the exile is not predicted as future, but presupposed as then existing; and while their statements are definite and accurate respecting what took place until near the close of the exile, all is vague beyond it, and has no correspondence with subsequent history. The real fact is that the character of these prophecies shows them to be predictive anticipation, and not historical reminiscence. They are not spoken out of the actually existing exile by way of descripton or retrospect, but out of the midst of foreseen tribulations and distresses. That these calamities are really future to the writer, and not past or present, is apparent from various considerations.

1. They are not specifically nor only the Babylonish exile. The expressions used are for the most part general, and are quite as applicable to other calamities and distresses. Thus, in chapters xl-lxvi the people are described as engaged in a warfare (xl, 2); passing through the waters and walking through the fire (xliii, 2); refined in the furnace of affliction (xlviii, 10); tossed with tempest (liv, 11); walking in darkness and having no light (l, 10); robbed, snared, and in prison (xlii, 22; xlix, 9); poor and needy, seeking water when there is none (xli, 17); a barren (liv, 1), forsaken (liv, 6), and divorced wife, or children sold to creditors (l, 1). The foes and oppressors of the people are described by terms equally general and indefinite; as, all that are incensed against thee and strive with thee (xli, 11; xlv, 24), that afflict thee (li, 23; lx, 14), that contend with and oppress thee (xlix, 25, 26); they are the islands, and peoples, and nations (xli, 1; xliii, 9; lix, 18), the uncircumcised and unclean (lii, 1). The period of oppression is subsequent to that by Egypt and Assyria, but not otherwise defined (lii, 4, 5). Captivity is referred to without saying where (li, 14), and a return to Zion without saying whence (li, 11). The allusion in xliii, 16-20, is to the exodus from Egypt, not from Babylon. The highway to be made in the desert (xl, 3) is not for the return of the people from exile, but of Jehovah to His people. Exiles are to return, not from Babylon merely, but from every point of the compass, and from the remotest parts (xliii, 5, 6; xlix, 12, as in xi, 11, which is acknowledged to be from Isaiah). God's work on their behalf is described as making the worm Jacob thresh mountains (xli, 14, 15), cleaving rivers in the desert (xli, 18), pouring water upon the thirsty (xliv, 3), planting trees in the wilderness (xli, 19), leading the blind, making darkness light, and crooked things straight (xlii, 16); bringing forth them that are in prison and in darkness (xlix, 9; li, 14); restoring the desolations

of Judah and Jerusalem (xlix, 8; li, 3; lii, 9; liv, 3), the everlasting wastes, the desolations of many generations (lviii, 12; lxi, 4)—expressions suggestive of more than an exile of seventy years.

Amid these general and far-reaching expressions, which perpetually recur throughout these chapters, the specific references to Babylon and Cyrus are few in number and limited in extent. Babylon and the Chaldeans are spoken of but three times outside of chapter xlvii, namely, xliii, 14; xlviii, 14, 20. Bel and Nebo, gods of Babylon, are mentioned once (xlvi, 1, 2). Cyrus is named in one passage (xliv, 28; xlv, 5, 13), and referred to four times besides (xli, 2, 3, 25; xlvi, 11; xlviii, 14, 15). With what propriety can these explicit references in a few passages to one great crisis in Israel's affairs be made to dominate the entire prophecy of twenty-seven chapters, and to restrict the application of numberless expressions occurring throughout, which in themselves suggest no such limitation? and a sense thus obtained, which is sometimes directly at variance with the language used, and which never adequately represents it, be held to justify the assertion that the Babylonish exile and deliverance from it is the one sole subject herein treated? and this to warrant the further inference, otherwise unsupported, that these chapters could have been written in no other period than that of the exile? The language of the prophet suggests that he is looking down over a future of gloom followed by brightness, into which desolation of the land, exile in Babylon, and deliverance from it enter, but which is indefinitely conceived, figuratively expressed, and which has a far wider and much more extensive meaning.

2. The impossibility of this limitation is further confirmed by the circumstance that another great event of the future is referred to with equal explicitness in these chapters. Another deliverer besides Cyrus is spoken of, the Servant of the Lord, whose function it is to open the blind eyes and to release the prisoners (xlii, 7; lxi, 1), to bless both Israel and the Gentiles (xlix, 6), to gather God's elect out of every land (xlix, 12), and by His vicarious sufferings to achieve a splendid triumph (chapter liii). Since the deliverance which He is to effect falls thus within the scope of this prophecy, the calamity described must likewise embrace that from which He rescues; and the happy issue depicted must include the glorious results which He shall accomplish. That superior stress is laid upon this ultimate and greater deliverance appears from the repeated declaration that there shall thenceforth be no further experience of suffering and woe (liv, 9, 10; lxii, 4-9; lxv, 19); while all that is glowing in human speech is summoned to describe the resulting exaltation and bliss of Zion (chapter lx), even to the creation of new heavens and a new earth (lxv, 17; lxvi, 22). Such language could

siah's reformation seems only to have made them self-righteous.

2. Consequent nearness of the divine judgment. God's forbearance had reached its last period. The Assyrians had passed off the scene. The Chaldeans are now charged with the execution of this sentence. They began as soon as good King Josiah died.

Three prophets in this period: Jeremiah, Habakkuk and Zephaniah. These occupy an unequal amount of space. From the long ministry of Jeremiah we have full account of his work. Prophecies of Habakkuk and Zephaniah are brief, as their ministries were. These books may be short, disconnected portions, or summaries of their prophecies. Of their persons we know nothing. The condition of things in Judah at this time was the same as that of Israel before the captivity, which called for the denunciations. There is this difference, however: (1.) The kingdom was not essentially criminal, nor utterly apostate. (2.) It still retained the body of God's people. (3.) The rejection, therefore, was not to be so great nor final. The kingdom looked at a future restoration, hence there is more room for promises, direct and indirect, positive and negative. While, therefore, Jeremiah is like Hosea, and Zephaniah like Amos, Habakkuk proclaimed the overthrow of Babylon is in contrast with Jonah. Jeremiah and Zephaniah are mainly denunciatory, with few promises. And so are most of the prophecies of this period. Habakkuk is chiefly consolatory. Judgment is necessary in order to break the fatal security of the people. For the sake of the people of God, in view of the great judgment it was important that the design and result of the judgment should be stated in advance. God was not to break off the covenant of grace, but his promises would still be fulfilled, Hab. 2:14; 3:13. (1.) Jeremiah had a long ministry, a large book of prophecy. The other books are short, and their ministries likewise. (2.) Full details of Jeremiah's life, while nothing is recorded of the others. (3.) Jeremiah and Zephaniah principally judgment on Judah, Habakkuk judgment on Babylon. (4.) Promises given that the judgment should not destroy but purify, limit set to the exile, people, city, kingdom, priesthood should not perish forever, Jer. chs. 31-33. The exile (Jer. 29:10), would be temporary. Every apparent loss should be more than compensated. Sequel to the preceding period in Judah. His promise was still to stand sure. The ark might perish, but would not be missed. Every loss was a real gain, Jer. 3 : 16, 17. The tables of the law might be lost, but the law was written on their hearts, Jer. 31 : 31–33. The Chaldean period is a sequel of what had preceded it. They were pursuing the same course with the same causes and similar results. The same judgment was still before them, but now nearer. (1.) The range of foresight of these prophets did not reach beyond that of the preceding ones. (2.) They reiterate the same predictions their predecessors proclaimed, often stating them in the same language. They thus conformed to the ancient prophecies, and at the same time give authority for their own predictions. (3.) No new or peculiar Messianic predictions. Habakkuk gives the negative side of the future, the overthrow of all that obstructs the people of God. Zephaniah is positive, and tells of the regathering of the people from captivity, and of their future glory. Jeremiah is both positive and negative, and at the same time goes beyond Habakkuk and Zephaniah, by introducing the person of Christ, as Branch of David, over Israel and Judah united. All three prophets declare that the theocracy is now to break up, and that all nations will one day be included in the kingdom of God.

JEREMIAH.

His life.—More details of Jeremiah's life are given than of any other canonical prophet. His name signifies " he whom God hath appointed," but the usage of the word makes it mean, " he whom God will throw down," and his was a ministry of overthrow and reconstruction, 1 : 10. He was son of Hilkiah, priest in Anathoth. He was, therefore, of priestly descent, like Ezekiel. Was Hilkiah the same as the one mentioned in 2 Kings 22 : 4 ? It is not certain, but probably they were different persons. For (1.) Jeremiah's father is never called the High-Priest. (2.) 1 Chron. 9 : 11 ; Nehemiah 11 : 11. The High-Priest, Hilkiah, was from Zadok, of the family of Eleazer, to whom this dignity was transferred, 1 Chron. 24 : 35 ; 1 Kings 2 : 35. (3.) In addition it has been alleged that the High-Priest must reside in Jerusalem. This is questioned. If the Hilkiah of Jer. 29 : 3, is the prophet's father, then the prophet had a brother. The hostility of his house against him is recorded in the

for Israel to the period succeeding the exile, in spite of so utter a lack of correspondence that no one at the time could ever have dreamed of their tallying, is the only ground for the assertion that the predictions of events after the captivity were not fulfilled, and for the conclusion thence strangely drawn, that they must have been written in the captivity.

3. There is an entire absence of anything to connect the writer himself with Babylonia. There is no suggestion of any locality there, or of any such surroundings as in the case of Ezekiel, who really did live in exile. There is repeated mention of Jerusalem and the cities of Judah (xl, 2, 9, etc.); Lebanon is used as an illustration, when a mountain is referred to (xl, 16); Ur of the Chaldees is spoken of as remote, at "the ends of the earth" (xli, 9); and the forms of idolatry described (lxv, 4sqq.) are those of Egypt, rather than those of Babylon, so that Ewald was led to conjecture that the writer was resident in Egypt.

4. There is a singular paucity of specific details respecting Babylon and Cyrus. Dr. Cheyne admits that Isaiah "might have learned almost as much about Babylon, as is mentioned in these chapters, either from traveling merchants or from the embassadors of Merodach baladan." And he adds, "This paucity of Babylonian references would be less surprising were it not for the very specific allusions to Palestinian circumstances in some of the later chapters." Cyrus is not even called the King of Persia, as in every historical reference to him in the Old Testament. He is simply a great conqueror from the north and east who should capture Babylon. But the whole description is general and ideal, with the exception of two remarkable circumstances, which none but a true prophet could have anticipated prior to their actual occurrence: that he should find the gates of Babylon open (xlv, 1), and that he should release the Jews and direct the rebuilding of Jerusalem and the temple (xliv, 28; xlv, 13.)

5. It is again and again declared that these statements respecting Cyrus were uttered before the event, before there were even any germinal indications of it (xli, 21-29; xlvi, 9-11, etc.). These are urged as the irrefragable proof of the divinity of Jehovah, and His superiority to idols, which possessed no such prescience. Such language is unaccountable if the prophet merely announced what was already obvious to sagacious observers. And it is besides fatal to the whole critical position. It is self-contradictory to say that a writer represents these events as taking place around him, and that his historical position is to be determined accordingly, while at the same time he alleges that the mention of them is evidence of divine prescience.

6. It is by no means true that the writer uniformly speaks as though the people were in exile. He speaks out of the actual present, Isaiah's own times, when he rebukes the people for seeking the alliance of foreign monarchs (lvii, 9), or for their neglect of the ritual worship (xliii, 23, 24; lxv, 11), or their hypocritical observance of it (lviii, 2-6: lxvi, 1, 3), or speaks of the temple as standing (lxvi, 6), and the regular service as performed there habitually (lxvi, 20), or of the punishment of the people as still future (xliii, 28, Revised Version; lxv, 6, 7, 12). The censures of idolatry (lvii, 3sqq.; lxv, 3, 4, 11; lxvi, 17) and the numerous arguments and warnings against it are, to say the

least, more in place in Isaiah's days than near the end of the exile. It is equivalent to a confession of the falsity of the assertion which the critics make on this subject, when Ewald alleges that paragraphs written before the exile have been interpolated into these prophecies; or Dr. Driver (*Isaiah*, page 188) supposes that the exilic prophet "borrows here passages written originally in the age of Jeremiah, and applies them to the generation of the exiles."

Again, the prophet transports himself not only to the time of the exile, but to that of Babylon's fall (xlvi, 1, 2), and the deliverance and glory of Israel (xl, 2; li, 3, Revised Version; lii, 9, 10, Heb.), and between the humiliation and glory of Messiah (chapter liii).

7. It cannot be satisfactorily explained how these disputed prophecies came to be included in the Book of Isaiah, if they are not really his. The later the date assigned to them, and the nearer to the time when the canon was collected, the more insupposable it becomes. And the complexity of the problem is increased by the fact that there is not merely one piece added at the end, but various pieces inserted at intervals in the course of the book; and this book is constructed upon a regular plan, into which these enter like the rest as component parts, and are essential to its symmetry and completeness. The assumption that these prophecies are by a "great unknown" is contrary to the analogy of the entire Old Testament, in which there is history and poetry by unknown authors, but no anonymous book of prophecy. Even the smallest of the minor prophets is kept distinct and referred to its proper author.

III. The objection from the alleged difference of style and diction is manifestly subordinate and precarious. It is a convenient species of argument, that in the hands of modern critics is always available to bolster up their foregone conclusions; and they abide by their own tests just so far as it may suit their purpose, and no further. The works of distinguished writers in modern times show differences quite as striking as any that exist in the Book of Isaiah. Whatever diversity there is is sufficiently explained by the admitted genius and versatility of the prophet; by the difference of occasion, subject, and purpose of the composition; and perhaps also by the more advanced period of his life. How little weight Dr. Cheyne himself attaches to the argument from diversity of style appears from his suggestion (*Commentary*, II, p. 230) that the author of chapters xl-lxvi "incorporated the substance of connected discourses of that great prophet, *of whose style we are so often reminded in these chapters—Isaiah.*"

The unity of the Book of Isaiah is vouched for by a steadfast tradition from the most ancient times and by the inspired authority of the New Testament. The doubts expressed as to certain portions are of recent origin, are traceable to an antisupernatural bias, and are supported by inconclusive arguments. The disputed portions are in harmony with the rest of the book, and with the revelations of Micah, a contemporary of Isaiah. They indicate by their character that they are a forecast of the future, not a description of the past and present; they contain no suggestion of the writer's presence in Babylonia; they are put forth as indisputably evidencing the divine foreknowledge; many passages are plainly preexilic; the

12th ch. 37 : 2, he had a cousin and an uncle. His uncle is said to be the same Shallum who was the husband of the prophetess Huldah, 2 Kings 22 : 14. Anathoth was established for the possession of the priests, Josh. 21 : 18. It was three miles north of Jerusalem. Here the prophet was born, 29 : 27, and spent his early years. He was called at an early age, 1 : 6. This was the year after Josiah began his first reformation. He was, therefore, called early to aid this pious king in his work. His youth may not have been so great as it seems to be from the expression, "a child," which is applied to him. This term is applicable from birth to twenty years of age, and is so used in other passages. We do not read that he ever acted as priest, and we know he was never married, 16 : 2. In the title of the book, 1 : 2, 3, mention is made of Josiah. But Jehoahaz and Jehoiakin are omitted. His ministry was forty years, to the capture of Jerusalem. Under Josiah, eighteen years, 13 : 31; Jehoash, three months; Jehoiakim, eleven years; Jehoiakin, three months; Zedekiah, fourteen years. Two remarks: (*a*) The omission of two of these kings made in Jeremiah, is accounted for either by the brevity of their reigns, or because nothing occurs to bring out anything from the prophet. (*b*) The ministry of the prophet is spoken of as extending only to the captivity of Jerusalem, whereas the prophecies of chapters 40–46 were after that date, Dan. 1 : 21.

Jeremiah's task was to testify of the coming ruin. He had done this for a long time. The kingdom was overthrown, and the people came into captivity. In order to complete the picture, he traces the fortunes of the remnant left behind in Jerusalem, and going from bad to worse. We are not to understand, therefore, that his ministry extended only to the captivity. Whatever he was to tell after this was not so important. Dan. 1 : 21, a parallel " until the first year of Cyrus;" but we find him after the third year of Cyrus. Yet the most important part of his ministry was before the first year.

Three great events. 1. The reformation of Josiah. 2. Capture of Jerusalem in the fourth year of Jehoiakim. 3. Its destruction in the eleventh year of Zedekiah. With the mention of 2 : 21 and 12 : 6 of the hostile treatment of the men of Anathoth, some have said he began his ministry in the place of his birth, but meeting with persecution there, went to Jerusalem. But 2 : 2 says he exercised his office in Jerusalem from the first, its vicinity being such that men of

Anathoth could exercise hostility toward him there easily. Was persecuted, 36 : 5 ; 22 : 2. The command, in 11 : 6, to the cities of Judah, does not say that his ministry was itinerant, because 26 : 2, he is represented as doing the same. No other prophet except Elijah met with such treatment. He was persecuted by others as well as by citizens of Anathoth. Even Elijah retired from persecution, Jeremiah kept on. He was warned of this when he was commissioned of God. He was met with sneers, 23 : 33–40. People upheld their false prophets, who attempted to destroy the force of Jeremiah's messages. The sight of this evil from the people of God was almost too much for such a prophet, and he 20 : 14–18, curses the day of his birth. It was not timidity, for no one can exceed him in courage, 20 : 11–13. His enemies were not confined to words, but extended to acts, 20 : 1–6, put in stocks by Pashur. Arrested on charge of treason 36 : 5, not imprisoned but under restraint. So that, 36 : 19, he could not with safety show himself. Ch. 29 : 26, 27, his punishment was demanded from Zephaniah. The prophet attempted to leave the city, 37 : 13. In spite of his denial of treason he was put in prison 26 : 8. Cast into a pit in the court of the prison to die, 39 : 15–18. His imprisonment must have lasted nine months. During this time Zephaniah consulted him secretly twice. Jeremiah came into Egypt when the Jews fled thence, and he remained there.

Legends concerning Jeremiah.—That he was stoned by the Jews, and that his grave is in Cairo. Alexandrian Jews loved him because he had been with them in Egypt, and they have many legends about him, 2 Mac. 2 : 1–7 ; 15 : 15, 16. From Matt. 16 : 14, it appears that at the time of Christ there was an expectation of his personal re-appearance, which may be accounted for by the fact that no mention is made of his death. Many think that he is one of the two witnesses in Rev. 11.

The Septuagint differs from A. V. very considerably. 33 : 14–26, have been dropped. 46 : 46–51 are not only in a different order among themselves, but the entire section has been removed to stand after ch. 26. These differences are remarked on by Jerome and Origen. Jerome—carelessness of transcribers. The Septuagint made from a faulty MS. Michaelis says there was one edition in Egypt after the prophet's death. From the nature of the variations it is evident that they cannot be traced to the ordinary differences in copying. They must have had a purpose.

writer transports himself in thought to postexilic as well as exilic times; the presence of spurious prophecies in the book cannot be accounted for; and there is no serious objection from style. Why then should we surrender our faith in Isaiah's authorship?

Text and Plan of Jeremiah.—Discrepancies between Hebrew and Greek text, abbreviations, additions, alterations, transpositions, remarked by Origen and Jerome. Theories of Egyptian and Palestine editions of the original. Due to the translator. (*a*) Their character; (*b*) inaccuracies and arbitrary changes in other books; (*c*) 2 Chron. 36 : 20. Prophecies not in chronological order. Hence many commentators complain of want of arrangement and confusion. Lightfoot and Blaney assume accidental dislocation. Eichhorn's hypothesis is that there were different editions of this book. (1.) These statements are based on a false assumption. The disorder claimed does not exist. (2.) These hypotheses are mere figments of the brain. The only solution they offer is a mere chance. (3.) Nothing can be safely built on the roll of Baruch, 36, because the contents of it are unknown. They were not for permanent preservation, but for a special occasion, 36 : 32. (4.) These theories regard the formation of the book as a mere mechanical work, thrown about without any ideas at all. This excludes any participation by the prophet in the arrangement of the book. Reaction in German criticism, and now Ewald recognizes an orderly arrangement.

The Book from Jeremiah Himself.—That the book in its present form proceeded from the prophet is shown: (1.) By the frequent use of the first person, both in the individual prophecies, and the headings of the transpositions, which show that he composed and arranged them, 12 : 6. (2.) In the fourth and fifth years of Jehoiakim, 36 : 2-32, he reduced to writing what had been given him. He was again told, 30 : 2, to write. That the prophetical book could not have been produced at the time is evident from the fact that these are productions after that time, and formulas of transition. The arrangement topical, hinted 27 : 12. Not written piecemeal in the course of his ministry, but a continuous composition prepared at its close. 1. Prophecies of different periods put together, those of the same period dispersed. 2. Prophecies accompanied by remarks made at a later period, 25 : 1. 3. Allusions to succeeding portions of the book. 4. Systematic disposition of the matter.

Analysis of Jeremiah.—Three sections with a historical appendix, ch. 52. I. chs. 1-33, Prediction of the judgment and the restoration. II. chs. 34-45, History of the judgment. III. chs. 46-51, Predictions respecting foreign nations. First section subdivided. A. chs. 1-20, General denunciation of Judah. B. chs. 21-23, Civil and religious leaders. C. chs. 24-29, Design and duration of the judgment. D. chs. 30-33, Blessing which would follow. Threatening preponderates, but a few words of promise in each division till the last. In A. not separate discourses, but continuous treatment of one theme; no date except 3 : 6. Second section. A. chs. 34-38, Evidences of ripeness for judgment. B. ch. 39, Destruction of the city. C. chs. 40-45, Fortunes of the remnant. No promise to the people, only one in each division to individuals, the Rechabites, 35 : 18, 19; Ebed-melech, 39 : 15-18; Baruch, ch. 45.

Contents of Jeremiah.—There is a larger number of symbols than in any previous prophet. The symbols are of three kinds.

Symbolic Visions.—Two occur in ch. 1 in connection with the call of the prophet and signify the character of his ministry. (*a*) 1 : 11, 12. " The rod of an almond tree," which God says means that he will hasten his word to perform it. It comes from a root meaning " to be awake." Thus God was about to waken to judgment. (*b*) 1 : 13, 14. "A seething pot and the face thereof is toward the north," which God says means that out of the north an evil shall break forth upon all the inhabitants of the land, *i. e.*, Babylon and its various sub-kingdoms were to desolate the land; these always entered Judah from the north. (*c*) 24 : 1-3, " two baskets of figs . . . one basket had very good figs even like the figs that are first ripe; and the other basket had very naughty figs, which could not be eaten, they were so bad." The good figs represented those that had just been carried away captive by Neb., for the captivity was to result in their good; and the evil figs represented those who remained in Judea under Zedekiah, for they were to suffer for worse evils. (*d*) 25 : 15, 16. A wine cup of which Jerusalem and all the nations were to drink—the fury of God in his judgment from which the nations were to be, as it were, intoxicated. This symbol is used by other prophets, and by Jeremiah elsewhere.

Symbolic Actions.—(*a*) Ch. 13 : 1-11. The prophet is directed to take a girdle and put it on his loins. Afterwards to hide it in a rock by the Euphrates. Then commanded to take it out and he finds it all spoiled. Explanation : Judah was bound to the Lord as a peculiar people, but they rebelled and now their pride was to be broken by the captivity. (*b*) 18 : 1-6. The prophet was directed to go down to the

potter's house, when he saw the potter make one vessel out of the clay, and that proving defective he made another. God could do with Israel as he pleased. (c) 19 : 1-13. The prophet was directed to take an earthen bottle and break it to pieces in the valley of Hinnom in sight of people and priests. Exp.—Judah was to be utterly destroyed. (d) 27 : 1-11, 12-22; 28 : 1-14. The prophet is directed to take yokes of wood and put them on his neck and send them to various nations. This is repeated in the reign of Zedekiah. Hananiah, a false prophet, breaks the yoke, whereupon the prophet is directed to make iron yokes and repeat the action. Exp,—Judah and these nations were to be brought under the rule of Babylon. (e) 32 : 6-15. The prophet is directed to purchase the field offered to him by his uncle's son, which he does, weighing out 17 shekels of silver, subscribing the evidence and sealing it in the presence of witnesses and recording the evidence of the purchase and putting all the papers in an earthen vessel. Exp.—Judah should be restored and reinherit her own land. (f) 35. The prophet is directed to set wine before the Rechabites, which he does, but they refuse to drink because of their father's command. Exp.—They regarded the command of their ancestor, though Judah did not recognize command of God and in consequence they were to be blessed and Judah punished. (g) 43 : 8-10. The prophet is directed to take great stones and to hide them in the clay in the brick-kiln, which is in Tahpanhes, in sight of the men of Judah. Exp.—Nebuchadnezzar should firmly establish his throne in Egypt and completely conquer the land. (h) 51 : 59-64. The prophet wrote in a book all the evil that was to come upon Babylon, and gave it to Seraiah who went into captivity along with Zedekiah and commanded him to read all that was written in it when he came to Babylon. After he had read it he should bind a stone to it and cast it into the Euphrates. Exp.—Babylon should be utterly destroyed.

Symbolic Names.—Passur, who persecuted the prophet and prophesied falsely, is called Magor-missabib. Fear round about. 20 : 1-6. Exp.—Refers to the terror and desolation to come upon him and the nation by the Babylonish captivity. Other names. Shallum, 22 : 11; Coniah, 22 : 24; new application of Jehoiakim and Zedekiah, 23 : 5, 6; Sheshach 25 : 26. Merathaim, Pekod, 50 : 21.

I. A. Ch. 1. introductory, describes character of his ministry, first literally, then symbolically, in two visions. Chs.

2-20, divided by headings into three parts. (1.) Chs. 1-6, argument of doom. (*a*) 2 : 1 ; 3 : 5 Judah guilty of forsaking Jehovah. (*b*) 3 : 6 ; 4 : 2 Judah worse than Israel. 8 : 14 Judah shall be brought back to Zion, and God will recognize His marriage relation to them on condition of their returning to Him. This will be fulfilled not in the return of the entire body, but even to single individuals. Instead of the foreign oppressors under whose sway they were, 3 : 15, they shall have pastors like David, 1 Sam. 3 : 14 ; Jer. 3 : 16. (*c*) 4 : 3 : 6 : 20, Judah to be visited by desolation and exile. (2) Neb. 7 : 13, Judah's covenant privileges could not save him. The ark of the covenant was to be destroyed even though Judah was relying upon it. God will reveal Himself to the pious among the people, in such a way as they had not experienced before. The whole city of God's people will be made what the ark had been before, v. 17. All nations would be gathered to Jerusalem. The promises of Jeremiah are substantially a repetition of those of Hosea and Amos. There are some differences however. (*a*) In Jeremiah there is an enlargement of God's grace. The condition of promise is more individual. (*b*) The announcement of Judah's fall is made with more distinctness, because the time of the evil was so much nearer. The speaking of the ark of the covenant as being taken away and destroyed implies a change in the whole economy. The ark had given value to the temple, and if that was gone, everything was lost, unless a new order of things should come in to take its place. A new dispensation here, and in ch. 31, was particularly appropriate because demolition was already about to take place. The taking away of the ark is not understood by those who think there will be a return to the rituals of Judaism, for what will they be without the ark? 2 Chron. 35 : 3. The prophet then goes on to say that Judah will be given into the hands of the heathen even as Israel was. The temple would not save them, 7 : 4 ; nor their sacrifices, 7 : 21 ; nor their possession of the law, 8 : 8 ; nor the presence of God, 8 : 19 ; nor their circumcision, 9 : 25, 26. Jeremiah 12 : 14-17 contains a promise to the Gentiles. God will return to them and bring them to His heritage. The form of this promise gives us a hint as to the literal method of interpretation. If this prophecy does not and cannot mean that the lineal descendants of Babylon shall be built up again in their own land, then why are we compelled to regard the promises in the case of Israel as literally a re-

turn to their own land? (3.) Chs. 14–20. Judah's doom terrible and inevitable. Yet there is a promise of distant mercy in a form implying the nearer judgment, 16 : 14, 15.

B. Chs. 21–23. The people having been sentenced, the prophet turns to the leaders of the people upon whom the guilt falls. He rebukes the kings of former days, and then contrasts with them the future faithful shepherds, and especially Messiah.

C. Chs. 24–29. Purpose and duration of the exile declared in the reign of Jehoiakim, " whom the Lord shall raise up." The former Jehoiakim was only a parody of the king who should come. Zedekiah, "the Lord' our righteousness." Here again the first is the mere parody of the second. Jeremiah concludes the first section of the book with a series of promises.

D. Chs. 30–33. These four chapters are promissory of blessings to follow the judgments; as appears from title of ch. 32. They are divided into two parts of two chapters each.

(1.) Chs. 30–31. 1. Ch. 30. (*a*) To both branches of the covenant people. (*b*) To the people separately. To Israel, 31 : 1–21. To Judah, 31 : 22–30. The promise is that they should be restored with David as their king. (2) The promise is that God will enter into a new and more intimate covenant relation with them than formerly when they came out of Egypt. And hence (31 : 31–34,) all shall know the Lord. The covenant written upon stone shall be engraved upon their hearts. The relation to the people shall be indissoluble, fixed as the natural laws of God, 31 : 35–37. (3.) These three truths, (*a*) the restoration, (*b*) the new intensity, (*c*) the perpetuity of the theocracy, having been stated in literal terms (31 : 38–40), are again set forth under a figure of the rebuilding of Jerusalem ; not only in its former dimensions, but greatly enlarged. It shall be rebuilt so as to extend over new territory outside, and formerly regarded as polluted, but now made sacred. Hill of Gareb, 31 : 39, the hill of the lepers, that profane spot outside of the city, where the lepers were banished. Goath (31 : 39): About the meaning of this there is a question. But the derivation of the word will decide it. It may be derived either from *gouh*, to expire, or *gaah*, to groan. It is probable that it denotes the place of execution of criminals. The temple is to include all these, and also, " the whole valley of dead bodies;" not the cemetery, but the valley of Hinnom, which was a very unclean place, and the image of hell. "And of the ashes." This place is the spot to which the ashes from the temple sacrifices were carried out of the city. "And all the fields unto the Brook of Kedron." These fields Josiah had defiled by strewing the ashes of the idolatrous vessels which had been burned upon the grass of the worshippers of the false gods, Baal and Astarte, 2 Kings 22 : 24-26. All these places were profane, yet to be included within the limits of the restored city, and to become holy to the Lord. Idolatry and pollution were not only not to come into the city, but the holiness of the city should reach out and hallow even that which before had been regarded as irretrievably unclean. That these promises do not belong to the material Jerusalem, nor to the natural Jerusalem as such, but to the spiritual people of God, is apparent, (*a*) from inspired application, Heb. 8 : 8 ; 10 : 15–17. (*b*) Also Jeremiah's words elsewhere. God's promises not bound by nationality irrespective of character, 18 : 6–10 ; the true Israel preserved in the faithful few notwithstanding the rejection of the unbelieving mass, 3 : 14 ; 24 : 4–10 ; and the building of heathen in the midst of God's people, 12 : 6 ; when the covenant of stone had been broken. God will put his law in their inward parts and write it in their hearts, 31 : 33. After the ark had been taken away (3 : 16), what is there to give sacredness to Jerusalem, which is not possessed by every other city which is spiritual? *Cf.* John 4 : 21–23.

(2) Chs. 32–33. Promises by restoration repeated, reaffirmed, and enforced by the symbol of the purchase of the field of Anathoth, outside the city. This indicates the certainty of a restoration. He then, in addition, gives : 1. Assurance of the perpetuity of royalty and priesthood (33 : 17–18). The purpose of God in this matter is as fixed as the succession of day and night. 2. The multiplication of those invested with royal and priestly dignity (33 : 22). Judah was on the point of being broken up and the temple destroyed, the throne of David cast down. But Jeremiah would teach the people of God that these things will not continue forever. A glorious future is before them. The theocracy is not dissolved, but only interrupted, to be restored again into a more glorious condition. The promise (33 : 17, 18), is that David and the priesthood should never lack successors. The marginal reading is the true rendering. This secures from extirpation, but not from temporary interruption. *Cf.* 2 Sam. 7 : 14–16 : Ps. 89 : 29–37, with Jer. 33 :

22. These promises are fulfilled in a three-fold way. (*a*) In a partial fulfillment in Zerubbabel, who, though not strictly king, exercised some regal functions. (*b*) Further fulfilled in Christ, who is the seed of David. (*c*) Finally in all the true people of God who are all to be made kings and adopted into the house of David. That this is intended appears from 33 : 22, where the vast multiplication of the house of David is mentioned. 1. The perpetuity of the kingdom does not require such a vast number of descendants. 2. Its fulfillment in the line of natural seed is not only not verified by fact, but would be preposterous and anything but a blessing. Therefore the Septuagint dropped this passage. A reigning family thus multiplied would be burdensome for the people to support. 3. The language of the promise is in the precise terms of that to Abraham. Therefore the entire family of Abraham is merged in the house of David. 4. This was the true idea of Israel, as the people of God. They were (Ex. 19 : 6) kings and priests. These functions for a time were entrusted to individuals, but were to revert to the people. 5. The N. T. teaches its fulfillment in all the people of God, 1 Pet. 2 : 9; Rev. 1 : 6; 5 : 10.

Priesthood.—There is an analogous fulfillment with respect to the priesthood. 1. Literal in the return from the captivity. 2. Christ as perpetual priest. 3. All the true people of God are priests, and are included in the family of Levi. That this last is included appears not only from the analogy of kingship but also because: 1. The thing really contemplated in the promise is that the priesthood should be *perpetual*. No stress was laid on its being in the fleshly family of Levi. The point at issue was not the prerogative of a tribe but the condition of the people. The office should remain. 2. Jeremiah often intimates the abolishment of the old economy, which implies a change of outward form. The ark of the covenant (3: 16) was to be taken away. This intimates the abolishment of the old economy of which the ark was the great representative. Ch. 31: 1–2 says a new covenant was to supersede the old covenant. 3. An older prophet speaks in like manner (Isaiah 66: 21; 61: 6) of the entire people of God. 4. From the providence of God. The priesthood of the tribe of Levi has never been literally perpetuated, and could not now be except by miracle, for all the tribal distinctions are lost. If the prophecy of Jeremiah is to meet with any fulfillment at all, it must be spiritual. 5. Teachings of N. T. 6. Even such a literalist as

Henderson confesses this. "We are shut up to the spiritual interpretation of this passage."

2. Chs. 34-45. A. 34-38, facts adduced as specimens and evidences of the prevailing corruption. Hebrew servants, ch. 34. Rechabites, ch. 35, Jehoiakim, ch. 36, Zedekiah chs. 37, 38. B. ch. 39, Destruction of city. C. chs. 40-45. The wretched remnant, closing with personal promise to Baruch.

3. Chs. 46-51. Probably in chronological order. Promises to Egypt, Moab, Ammon and Elam; none to Babylon, 51 : 65. Ch. 52, historical appendix, perhaps added by another. (1.) Jer. 51 : 64. (2.) Similar narrative in ch. 39. (3.) Date of 52 : 31-34, twenty-six years after the destruction of the city. (4.) Coincidence with 2 Kings. Contains no mention of return from exile. Jeremiah's adoption of language of preceding books, especially ch. 48, Moab; 49: 7, etc., Edom; affords incidental proof of their genuineness; variations not arise from corruption of text.

LAMENTATIONS.

One of the five Megilloth, in Hagiographa or after Jeremiah, catalogues of canon. Hebrew, Greek and Latin names. Not composed with reference to death of Josiah, 2 Chron. 35: 25, nor on occasion of his death with foresight of destruction of city, but on occurrence of this latter event. Five sections of one chapter each; all alphabetical but the last; ch. 3, triple recurrence of each letter; chs. 2, 3, 4, transposition of Ayin and Pe. Not distinct elegies relating to successive states of Jerusalem's overthrow. Written by Jeremiah, (a) unanimous voice of tradition, verse prefixed in Septuagint and Vulgate, Josephus, Origen, Jerome, Talmud, (b) correspondence with character of prophet, coincidences of statement of facts and forms of expression, (c) no ground for disputing it.

HABAKKUK.

Of the present and personal circumstances of the prophet we know nothing except from his book. It is inferred from 3: 19, his last words, that he was of the tribe of Levi, and one of the family engaged in sacred music of the temple.

This is plausible, and if true, it gives a real explanation of the close resemblance of ch. 3 to the Psalms, and the adoption there of so many technical terms which belong to the Psalms. The title of ch. 3, and the subscription are both modeled after the Psalms. Selah occurs three times; and the last verse is almost verbatim from the Psalms. If this be held, it would be another instance of prophets taken from the temple servitors. Jeremiah, Zechariah, and Ezekiel were priests. While the prophets of the former period were independent of the sacred orders, in this degenerate age the fittest material was found among the priests.

The date of the prophet is inferred from. 1. That the invasion of the Chaldeans would be in the lifetime of that generation, 1: 5, 6. Hence not in the reign of Josiah. 2. Chap. 2: 20 implies that the temple was standing. Musical worship still continued in the temple (3: 19). This was probably after the twelfth year of Josiah's reign. Hence Habakkuk was a contemporary of Jeremiah and Zephaniah, and not more than 24 years before the invasion of Nebuchadnezzar. 3. The order of minor prophets. Some try to fix the date more exactly, by comparing it with Jeremiah and Zephaniah. Thus, it is said, that as Jeremiah is much more specific as to the Babylonian conquest, while Habakkuk mentions only the bare fact, therefore Habakkuk was before Jeremiah. This is sometimes the case, but not always, and therefore cannot be made the basis of argument. Sometimes it is reversed, *e. g.*, Isaiah prophesied the overthrow of Babylon more minutely than did Habakkuk. Again, there are passages in which Jeremiah and Zephaniah have borrowed the language of Habakkuk. Yet while this is probably true, the argument as to priority is questionable, because it can be so easily reversed. The design is both minatory and consolatory. Minatory to chastise sinners in Judah; consolatory to comfort the pious.

The prophecy of the overthrow of Babylon. Observe: I. Its dramatic power. First he speaks to God for the people. Then God answers. Then the prophet speaks for himself. Then God speaks to the prophet. Finally he gives utterance to his prophecies of joy. What is peculiar is this regular alternation from beginning to end, and is an index of the psychological condition of the prophet. He is in a rapt, ecstatic state, and the form of the prophecy reproduces his own states of mind; and the dramatism is not merely a form, or due to fancy, but is what really took place, like the

visions of other prophets. The prophet is not an artist, but
a seer. But this ecstacy does not supersede his natural
faculties, but lifts them to a higher sphere. The fact is, the
prophetical inspiration has its analogy with spiritual illumination.
A real supernatural communication is made *ab
extra*. Yet the extraordinary method attaches itself to the
ordinary methods used by the Holy Spirit. The facts revealed
are not absolutely new truths. The unknown is
imparted as limited with what was previously understood,
and a sense of need is created which demands the new truth;
and thus God revealed His purpose that the land should be
ravaged by the Chaldeans, and they in turn overthrown.
But this was disclosed as part of the spiritual training of the
people, and hence given in their moral senses and relations.
Judah was very corrupt. Fraud and impiety were unchecked.
God's law was disregarded. Shocked by this, and personal
wrongs, the pious, through Habakkuk, appeal to God if He
will longer tolerate it. They are in extremity and look up
to God. Then the answer comes in a revelation adapted to
this state of need. God will punish by the Chaldeans. But
with this come fresh doubts and difficulties. The fear lest
the fierce Chaldeans should involve in punishment the good
and bad together. Hence they appeal to God again; and
plant themselves upon His attributes and covenant relations.
They cling to the conviction that the Chaldean invasion was
for correction and not for destruction. They appeal to God
as governor of the world. Thus the new complexities of
Providence demand fresh solutions, and the prophet waits
the answer. It then comes. The Chaldeans themselves
shall be trodden down, and the people abide the retribution
of Jehovah. And hence the people of God are prepared for
vengeance in the same way in which they are ever prepared
for new supplies of grace. But while this is true, we must
not confound the two methods. Here there is a real disclosure
of truth. The prophet does not *infer* a judgment on
themselves and upon the Chaldeans, and then announce
these results; but he had a divine revelation necessitating
his belief. We have the same general providence to guide
us, but we can not so supply it as to make it reveal the
future. Hence there was a real revelation, and not a mere
inference; which would be conjectural, delusive, and unfulfilled.
Still less is it a *vaticinium post eventum*. Nor is it a
declaration of what was so near as to be within the power of
human foresight. On the contrary the prophets declare that

they would not believe it though it were told them. And the fact of the overthrow of Babylon could not be calculated upon. Hence the future is disclosed, not as mere disjointed facts, but as the laying bare of the links which bound the future to the present. This lays the foundation of the *propheticum curriculum* a common track which all pursue. They proceed from a charge of sin to its penalty. And if in reference to God's people, they proceed to fact of deliverance. Observe these especially in Habakkuk. He begins with the sins in Judah; passes to their punishment by the Chaldeans; and then to the overthrow of Babylon. While it is a revelation it is not merely an anticipation of history. The prophet is true in representing the future; yet the prophet so surveys it from his own view that it is good evidence that it is prophetical and not historical. Hence it is written from the prophet's own historical standpoint, and by its structure indicates its own prophetic truth.

Divisions of the Book.—The first complaint, 1: 2-4. The Lord's response, 1: 5-11. The second complaint, 1: 12; 2: 1. The Lord's response, 2: 2-20. The triumph, ch. 3. The injustice and oppression in Judah to be punished by the Chaldeans and the Chaldeans to be punished by their overthrow. The burden, 2: 4-20, consisting of a brief preamble and five woes in successive stanzas. Messianic passage in the third. Ch. 3 a lyrical recapitulation, resemblance to the Psalms in style, artistic form, title, subscriptions and Selah. Applied by the fathers to the advent and work of Christ. Bengel's chronological hypothesis, v. 2; vs. 3-15 not historical; (*a*) diversity in the explanation of details; (*b*) disproportionate length; (*c*) tense of opening verb, v. 3 (Hebrew). Prophetic of a divine descent to judgment, which is to include whatever was most grand in former manifestations of God, directed against the Chaldeans and all other foes. Convulsions of nature poetic and emblematic or suggestive of the final judgment.

ZEPHANIAH.

Habakkuk describes judgment on Chaldeans; Zephaniah a universal judgment, in which, however, no allusion is made to the Chaldeans, who are viewed, not as objects, but as executioners of God's wrath. It has special reference to the unfaithful in Judah, and inferior contiguous nations, from whose fate, as in Amos, an argument of Judah's doom is derived, 3: 6-8. Zephaniah and Jeremiah more frequent allusions to former Scriptures than Habakkuk. Zephaniah's ancestry traced through four degrees, to Hezekiah, probably the king, (*a*) identity of name; (*b*) traced to so remote an ancestor; (*c*) correspondence with the date. Objections that he is not explicitly called king, and that no such son of king Hezekiah is mentioned in the history. Date, 1: 1, probably after Josiah's twelfth year. Other criteria inconclusive; 2: 13, predicted desolation of Nineveh; 1: 4, "remnant of Baal," cutting off Chemarim; 1: 8, "the king's children;" 3: 4, "the law." Ch. 1, universal and sweeping judgment, with particular application to the wicked in Judah, vs. 4–13; exhortation to seek the Lord as the only means of escape 2: 1–3; enforced by judgments on other nations, exhibited in three stanzas, of four verses each, Philistia in the west, Moab and Ammon in the east, Ethiopia and Assyria in the south and north. In the middle stanza, Messianic allusion, as in Habakkuk. Application to Jerusalem, 3: 1–8. Promissory conclusion, vs. 9–20. The heathen shall possess a pure language, and take part in the restoration of God's people. Purity and blessedness of Israel.

PERIOD OF THE EXILE.

The course of degeneracy was now violently terminated. It was followed by a period of seclusion and trial. In order to effect the best results in this process, they were, first, to be sifted, the best carried away, the worst left to perish in Jerusalem. The good figs indicate those carried into exile. The sifting was performed: 1. By the overruling providence of God; 2. Natural causes. The Lord had told the people by Jeremiah what was to come. Those who believed the prophecy would be submissive, (*a*) to the disposition of the people; (*b*) to the intentions of the Chaldeans.

Two things were needed in this period. 1. Influence upon the people themselves; 2. Influence upon the oppressors in behalf of the people. The former was exerted by Ezekiel; the latter by Daniel. Ezekiel dwelt among the exiles for their instruction, comfort and elevation. Daniel lived at the court of Babylon to protect the interests of the people, and to consult for their welfare as Joseph did before

Pharoah. Hence Daniel is placed in the Hagiographa. The work needed was of two kinds, according to the period. The first part of the exile was a transition period, during which there was the mere shadow of a kingdom. The exile began in the fourth year of Jehoiakim. This portion of the period of the exile, therefore, overlaps the former, the Chaldean. Ezekiel, therefore, was living contemporaneous with Jeremiah. His ministry was fitted to the period. As long as Jerusalem still stood, the false prophets indulged presumptuous hopes; and hindered the growth of that humility and penitence which the captivity was designed to produce. Hence his discourses were denunciatory, and full of warning, during this time. After the city had actually been destroyed, a ministry of consolation was needed to preserve the people from utter despair. Up to the fall of Jerusalem his ministry was like that of Jeremiah, but afterwards it entirely changed

Ezekiel and Daniel.—(*a*) Ezekiel was to build up the theocracy from within, Daniel was to exhibit the kingdom of God in its conflict with, and victory over, the enemies of God. Both use figures. (*b*) Ezekiel draws his symbols mainly from the sanctuary with which his position as priest made him familiar. Daniel draws from other sources. (*c*) There is the same variety in Messianic predictions. Ezekiel sometimes sets them forth from a priestly point of view. Daniel exhibits it as the universal and unending empire of the Son of Man. These prophets note the exact time in which their prophecies were recorded, and sometimes the very month. Ezekiel, 24:1-2, tells the fact of the siege of Jerusalem the very day it began. The exile was the conclusion of God's dealings with the Jews. The prophets preceding the exile were limited to the judgments wrought by or upon Babylon. Now they pass from the Babylonish exile to the future troubles of Israel, and the succession of empires, until the Messiah, and the conversion of the world. When the exile was at hand, it was necessary to prepare the people for coming events, lest they should suppose that, with the exile, all was lost. This opinion it was necessary to correct, by showing that a long period must intervene, succession of empires, and times of trouble come, before the advent of the Messiah.

EZEKIEL.

Fewer details are given of Ezekiel than of Daniel. His work was spiritual, and the events of his life had no special effect upon his work. The record of his life is found in his prophecy.

Name.—" One whose God strengthens him." He was carried captive eight years after Daniel with Jehoiachin. His ministry began (ch. 1:1) in the fifth year of Jehoiachin's captivity, (this event dated from rather than Zedekiah's reign), the year after Jeremiah's message, Jer. 51:59, in the thirtieth year of his age, Num. 4:3. During the early portions of his ministry, he was a contemporary of Jeremiah thirty years. This was not from the first year of Nabopolassar, nor from the last jubilee, nor the eighteenth year of Josiah. 1. There is no proof that these were eras. 2. There is no other date reckoned from them. 3. If intended they would have been mentioned.

Scene of Labors.—3:15, at Tel-abib, by the Chebar, same as Habor, 2 Kings, 17:6. Marriage, 24:18.

Duration of Ministry.—Uncertain. 29:17, is the latest date of the book, the twenty-seventh year of Jehoiachin's captivity. The people were hopeful and yet rebellious. But the effect of his labors was shown by: 1. Frequent consultation by elders and others, 8:1; 14:1. 2. Freedom in uttering his reproofs; 3. Moral changes effected during the exile. His Hebrew has more anomalies and foreign forms than that of Daniel, who was both Hebrew and Chaldee. This corruption is first found in Jeremiah. It was natural that the change of language should affect the dialect of the people.

Divisions of the Book.—**1.** Before the capture of Jerusalem, chs. 1–24, denunciatory. **2.** Respecting foreign nations, chs. 25–32. **3.** After the capture of Jerusalem, chs. 33–48, promissory. Opening vision, 1:1; 3:15, like Isa. 6 and Rev. 4, based on cherubim over the ark. Design not merely to make an impression of majesty and glory but as preparation for this specific message. The Mosaic symbol its general signification. The God of creation and of temple present in profane land of captivity, and about to make a communication to the prophet. Modifications, its particular application; (*a*) life and swiftness; (*b*) fire, wrath, qualified by rainbow of the covenant. Verbal commission and symbol of roll, 2:9; 3:3, *cf.* Rev. 10:9. After seven days, con-

nected prophecy to end of ch. 7: Responsibilities of his office, four symbolic actions followed by denunciation in literal terms; (a) tile, besieged city; warfare; (b) lie bound 390 and 40 days. Literal performance physically impossible, out of proportion to the end, weaken the impression, chronological difficulty. Not represent days of siege, with which they do not correspond, and the days stand for years, 4: 6, either of sin or punishment; how reckoned, (c) bread, (d) hair. Chs. 8–11, one year later. Presumption of inhabitants of Jerusalem; effect on exiles. 1. The crimes of Jerusalem and its certain destruction, 8: 1; 11: 13. 2. The exiles are God's true covenant people, 11: 14–21. Profanation of temple, not perhaps actual, scenes of single idolatrous festival, or various forms of idolatry gathered there, but ideal concentration. (a) Lev. 16: 16–19; (b) Ex. 20: 3; (c) temple was Judah's place of worship; (d) justified by actual profanation at different times. Image of jealousy, chamber of imagery, Jaazaniah, Tammuz, five and twenty men. Six men with the man in linen. Five and twenty men at the east gate, Pelatiah, son of Benaiah. Promises to exiles. (a) God will be a sanctuary to them, 11: 16; (b) bring them back to land of Israel, v. 17; (c) give them a new heart, v. 19. Glory of God forsakes the temple. Denunciations continued until the day that Jerusalem is besieged, ch. 24. Seven foreign nations, chs. 25–32. Ammon, Moab, Edom, Philistia, Tyre, Zidon, Egypt. Promises: I. Deliverance from foes, chs. 33–39. II. Restoration of the theocracy, chs. 40–48. I. Evening preceding news of fall of city, second formal call of prophet, ch. 33; deliverance from wicked rulers, David their shepherd, ch. 34; from present foes, Edom denounced, contrasted blessedness of Israel, valley of dry bones, union of the two sticks, chs. 35–37; from future foes, Gog and Magog, chs. 38, 39. II. Fourteenth year after the city was smitten, 1st month and 10th day.

Different Opinions.—1. Historical, of what had been. 2. Mandatory, for the direction of the exiles. 3. Prophetic, It can not be literal. 1. Historical, for (a) it did not correspond with what had been; (b) unnecessary if it referred to the past; (c) the language prevents such reference. 2. It is not mandatory, because the exiles did not follow the commands. 3. It can not be prophetic, for this would be contrary to the declarations of N. T. and the intimations of O. T. If prophetic, it would predict the return of the Christian church to Jewish forms, but the Jewish ritual is abolished by the sacrifice of Christ and the providence of God. It is symbolic and ideal, for: 1. The original temple was symbolical: made use of symbolically by Ezekiel elsewhere, Jer. 31: 38-40. 2. It yields a good and proper sense. 3. There are many things in the vision which could not be carried out literally, *e. g.*, the size of Jerusalem and the temple; the stream proceeding from the temple and healing the nations. 4. It is like Rev. 21: 22. In fact Rev. seems to be a commentary on this passage. Rev. is symbolic.

2 40-48. This last vision was at the beginning of the year (40: 1). These chapters contain 1. Description of the temple. 2. Ritual service in the temple; 3. final apportionment of the land. Some take literal views, others regard the temple as ideal.

This section is divided: (1.) 40-43: 12, Measure of the temple. The church of God is to be re-established on the earth. Ezekiel's temple in the vision differs from Solomon's real temple, (*a*) in dimensions, which are enlarged, (*b*) Ezekiel gives more prominence to subordinate facts. Nothing is left to the choice or direction of the builders. . He gives a great deal of time to the gates, the doors, the courts, etc. These inferior parts have a new and sacred importance connected with them. The court is exalted to a sacred preeminence corresponding to the Holy of Holies in Solomon's temple, 43: 1. In the new temple the glory of God is never to depart. In the old it did, 11: 23. (2.) 43: 13; 47: 12. This division gives a description of the holy service. Priests, people and rulers should all be united in the worship, 47: 1-12. The trees by the stream of life remind us of Paradise. To represent the blessings brought by this stream it is spoken of as flowing to dead localities, even to the Dead Sea, which shall be purified, the Dead Sea being the symbol of all that is vile and lifeless. Even this shall be vitalized and beautified by this stream of life. The only places not reclaimed are those not reached by this stream. (3.) 47: 13; 48: 35. Concluding Portion, Division of the land among the twelve tribes. Two points of difference from the real division. (*a*) Uniformity of division. All have an equal portion from W. to E., and all are on the W. side of the Jordan. No tribe is preferred above another, 47: 22, 23; Rev. 7: 5-8. It is even said that strangers dwelling among them shall have equal privileges. (*b*) Ezekiel's division leaves nothing to the decision of men, but all fixed by God. We can not conclude that the Christian church is ever to

return to Judaic forms. This last portion shows how O. T. forms may set forth N. T. things.

DANIEL.

The name signifies "God's judge," *i. e.*, "one who delivers God's judgments." According to 1:1, Daniel was of the tribe of Judah, and of princely descent. He was carried away in the first deportation by Nebuchadnezzar, eight years before Ezekiel. Carried away at the beginning of the exile, he survived its close, but did not return, probably because of advanced age. He was a favorite of Nebuchadnezzar on account of his wisdom and supernatural endowments, which are referred to by Ezekiel, chs. 14:14; 28:3. He was set aside by Belshazzar, and reinstated by Darius. The ministry of Daniel was mainly external, in reference to the kingdoms of this world in conflict with the kingdom and people of God.

Divisions of the Book.—1:1-6. Personal history of Daniel and his friends, historical. 2:7-12. National, prophetical visions. The book does not profess to be a history of the exile, or a connected biography of Daniel, but a series of pictures of exile life. 2:4; 7:28, is in Chaldee; the rest of the book is in Hebrew. The number and greatness of its miracles mark it out as a special object of hostility to skeptics. Celsus and Porphyry, English deists and German rationalists, have attacked it, and the book has been referred to the time of the Maccabees. The best treatise in reply to the following objections is Hengstenberg's "Authenticity of Daniel."

Objections.—1. Greek words: (*a*) their number exaggerated; (*b*) readily accounted for; (*c*) like charge against still older books of Bible; (*d*) abandoned as untenable. 2. Position in canon. (*a*) Division of canon not chronological; (*b*) Jewish tradition; (*c*) accounts for nothing, true explanation. 3. Needless multiplication of miracles. But (*a*) needed by people; (*b*) prepared the way for their restoration; (*c*) present effect on the heathen; (*d*) future consolation. 4. Definite dates and minute details of the prophecies. (*a*) Naturalistic views; (*b*) explicitness of other prophecies, 70 years' captivity, 65 years Ephraim, 3 years Moab, 15 years Hezekiah, fall of Babylon, Zechariah 9:13, same conflict with kingdom of Greece; (*c*) provide for the future wants of the people. 5. Definite predictions only to death of Antiochus; (*a*) like limitation in other prophecies, Jacob, Isaiah, Jeremiah, Ezekiel, Zechariah; (*b*) date of Messiah's advent, rise of Roman empire. 6. Self-laudation, but (*a*) so Moses, Paul; (*b*) impartiality of sacred writers; (*c*) Daniel relates facts or repeats words of others. Proofs of genuineness. 1. Purports to have been written by Daniel; 1st person in second part, and unity of the whole shown by consistent plan, like expressions, reciprocal allusions, change of language; can neither be fiction nor fraud. 2. Canon closed in time of Ezra and Nehemiah. 3. Our Lord Son of Man, kingdom of heaven, Mat. 24 : 15, 30; 26 : 64; John 5 : 28, 29; Apostles Heb. 11 : 33, 34; 1 Cor. 6 : 2; 2 Thes. 2 : 3; 1 Pet. 1 : 10–12, Revelation. 4. Josephus, 1 Macc., Greek version. 5. Character of the Hebrew, of the Chaldee, use of both languages as in Ezra 6. Acquaintance with the history, shewn in character of Daniel, Nebuchadnezzar, Darius, Belshazzar, no error in dates, Nebuchadnezzar's adorning Babylon, prophetic dream, insanity, circumstances of Babylon's capture, Darius the Mede, 120 princes, Medes and Persians, Persians and Medes. 7. Knowledge of customs; land of Shinar, 3 : 2, fed from king's table, changing names of Daniel and his companions, years of Nebuchadnezzar's reign, punishments, colossal image, music, women at entertainments, gold chain, king's edicts immutable, the magi. 9. Abundance of symbols as in Ezekiel; book inconsistent with assumed Maccabean origin.

Prophecies.—The disclosures in the second and seventh chapters are parallel. The second chapter has Nebuchadnezzar's dream—four empires, Babylon, Medo-Persia, Macedon, Rome. The seventh chapter contains the vision of the four beasts=the same four empires. The lion with eagle's wings=Babylon. The bear with three ribs=the Medo-Persian; greedily ravenous propensity. The leopard with four wings and four heads=the Macedonian Empire, portioned into Syria, Egypt, Thrace and Macedon. A nondescript animal with ten horns and a little horn=the Roman empire, whose attack no animal is fierce enough to withstand. Ten horns indicate ten successive kings, and the little horn=Antichrist. St. John sees only one beast, which represents all Daniel's beasts in one. The seven heads of John's beast represent the seven empires in which one ungodly power was embodied. The Apostle says five had already existed, Egypt, Assyria, Babylon, Syria, Macedon.

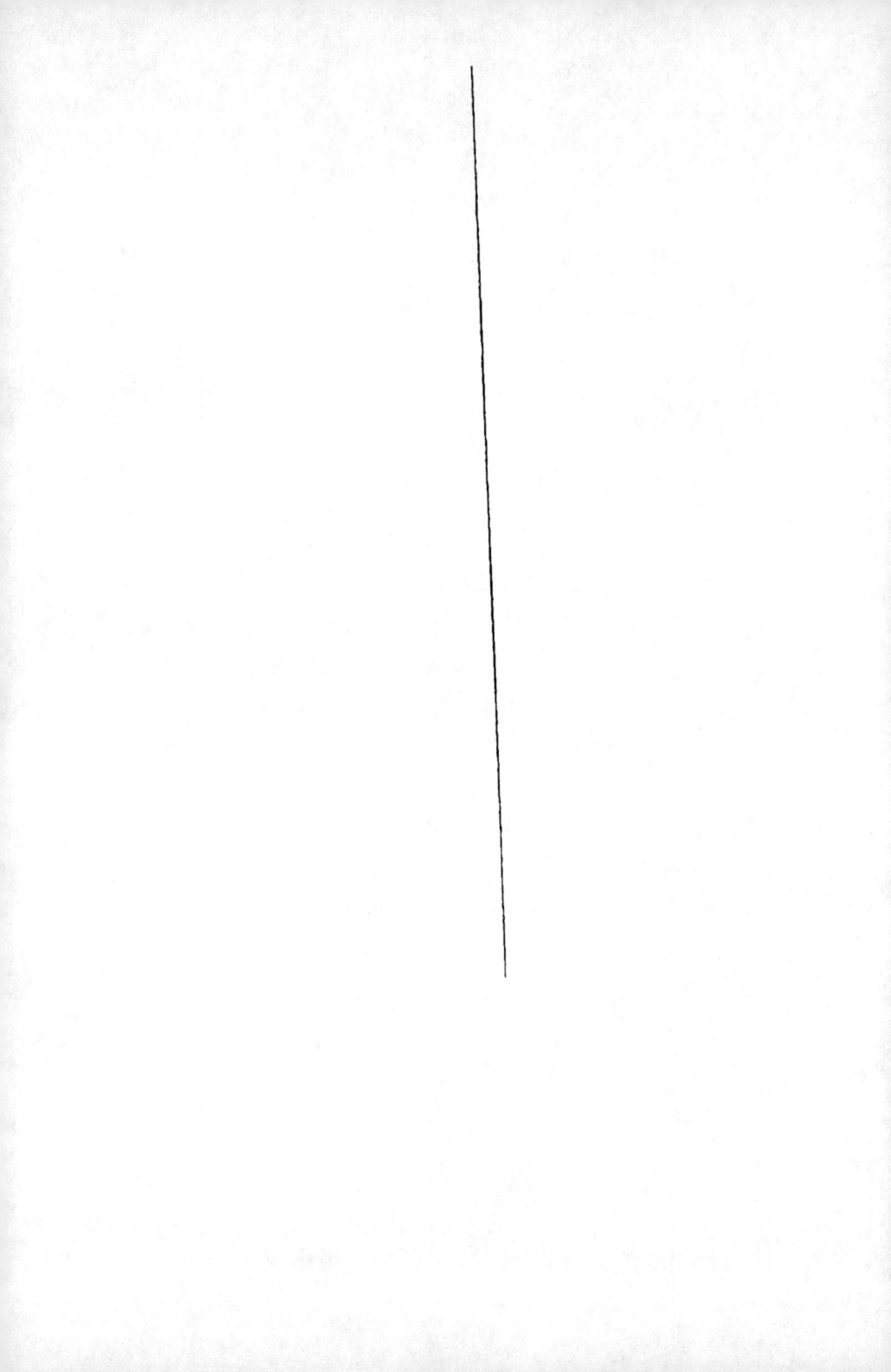

The one standing in Rome. Another is yet to come. The interpretation so depends on historical facts that all orthodox writers agree as to its meaning. Skeptics have invented other meanings for symbols. They are, 1. To divide the Medo-Persian empire into two. But (*a*) this was only one. Media and Persia was the same empire. Persians were confederated with the Medes, the only change being that of the reigning family. (*b*) It is always thus spoken of by profane and sacred writers; Esther; Daniel 5: 28; 6: 8; 12: 15. (*c*) The skeptics make the leopard represent the Persian empire; but the leopard has four heads, and Persian empire was not so divided. 2. To divide the Macedonian empire into two, Babylonian, and Medo-Persian, the Macedonian empire of Alexander, and those of his successors being made separate. But (*a*) the leopard with four heads represents the empire broken into four parts. (*b*) The fourth empire is stronger and more terrible than its predecessors, *cf.* 8: 22; 11; 4. (*c*) Then no explanation would be given of the ten horns.

Chs. 8–12 are supplementary. In chap. 8, the ram=Syria. The he-goat=the Macedonian empire. The horn between his eyes=Alexander the Great. The four horns springing up=Syria, Egypt, Thrace, Macedon, into which the empire was divided at Alexander's death. Out of the Syrian kingdom grew a little horn which waxed greater. This was Antiochus Epiphanes who was monarch of the kingdom, the persecutor of the Jews.

Ch. 9, revealed in the first year of Darius the Mede, which is the 69th year of the captivity. The prophet was praying for the restoration of the people when further, full disclosures were made to him. It might be supposed that immediately, at the expiration of the captivity, the kingdom of the Messiah would come. But the angel tells the prophet that the seventy weeks are about gone, but that there are yet to come seventy more years to finish the transgression by atonement. All relates to the work of Christ. Within these seventy weeks of years, all these Messianic functions shall be performed. This is made more precise by dividing these seventy weeks into three periods of seven, sixty-two and one weeks. He informs us from what point of time the seventy weeks are to date, viz., the going forth of the commandment to rebuild Jerusalem. This is not the permission of Cyrus to return to their own land. Down to the time of Nehemiah, the city was still in runs, Neh. 2: 3. The first effectual measures were taken by him, after that he received permission to rebuild, Neh. 2: 5, 6, in the twentieth year of Artaxerxes Longimanus. This is the exact time from which the seventy weeks were to begin. There is some difference among historians as to the length of Artaxerxes' reign. Hengstenberg goes into an elaborate argument to show that the time of the prophecy was exact. The entire restoration of the city would be accomplished though in the midst of much trouble. After sixty-nine weeks would be the Messiah's public appearance; in the midst of the last week. His effectual sacrifice, followed by destruction of the city and sanctuary. What distinctly belongs to the last week is shown in 9: 27.

Chs. 10-12. The last vision of the book. In the third year of Cyrus, Daniel was in mourning because of the events in Ezek. 4: 1-5. The subject of ch. 8 is here resumed and dwelt upon in literal language. Prediction in literal terms of the overthrow of the Persian empire by Alexander. Division of his empire at his death! Persecution of Antiochus set forth. As a relief from these dark pictures he gives the brightness of the future, the resurrection and external glory. Reluctant testimony of skeptics to the truth of the prophecies. Apocryphal sections are added in the Septuagint.

PERIOD OF THE RESTORATION.

The period of captivity is now over. The decree has been procured from Cyrus that the Jews may return to their own land. Ezekiel has prepared the people inwardly for their return, and for the establishment of the forms of the theocracy. The people had been sifted at the close as at the beginning of the exile. The work of Ezekiel and Daniel had been amongst this better class. It was the better and more pious people who would leave their houses and return to Jerusalem to rebuild that desolated city. Returning to their own land, new opposition meets them from the Samaritans, and other enemies. The exiles were under strong temptation, therefore, to succumb to despair. Haggai and Zechariah cheer them under present trials and discouragements, by showing: 1. That their present weakness was no indication that God was not with them. For in spite of present adversities they should rise higher than ever before. They were shown also that the heathen nations should be brought low, and pour in their resources to them; Ezra

し　ご　い　お

5:1; 6:14. 2. The altered condition and disposition of the heathen nations. Haggai and Zechariah appear to be summoned to the prophetic office within one month of each other, and they labored together. The book of Zechariah, indeed, seems to be an expansion of the smaller one of Haggai. It was the mission of both to show the people that their present condition was due to temporary causes, and should not last forever. But in comforting the people, and in promising them that there was danger that they would think the glory was to come immediately, Zechariah prepares them for additional troubles before the promises should be fulfilled, and declares how signally they would be delivered out of them. He dwells chiefly on the external condition of the people.

Malachi is different. The people must not think that the divine blessing would be given to them without regard to their own character. The altered tones of the prophecies grew out of the different circumstances in which they were uttered. The ministry of Malachi was later than that of Zechariah and Haggai; and the temple had been built, but the long years of suffering had brought to light certain evil tendencies. It had shown a measure of hypocrisy. These must be removed if they would enjoy the blessings which the older prophets had predicted. Thus we have the O. T. prophets forming themselves into a grand scheme, and each period forming the preparation for that to come. The prophets are, therefore, not isolated individuals, but are to carry forward from age to age one divine scheme.

HAGGAI.

The name signifies "a feast." A relation has been found or fancied in the fact that he labored for the restoration of the feast of the Jewish rituals. He is mentioned in Ezra 5:1; 6:14. The *duration of his ministry* is unknown. The discourses in his book were all delivered within four months. It would be precarious to say from this that his ministry lasted only four months, as it would be, from Ezra 6:14, to say that it lasted through the entire reign.

Four discourses.—The dates of all which are accurately given. It is not probable that these are the only discourses he ever uttered. They are the only ones for the benefit of the church in the time to come. Cyrus had no sooner died, than the adversaries obtained from the king decrees adverse to the building of the temple. Haggai strives to waken them to courage, to the rebuilding of the temple. These discourses were delivered in the second year of Darius.

1. The first (ch. 1) was addressed to Zerubbabel, governor of Judah, and to Joshua, the high-priest, Hag. 1:1. It reprimanded them for the suspension of the building of God's house, while they content themselves with dwelling in their own houses. He urges them to go at once and bring wood to build the house. The effect was that the people began that same month to build.

2 The second discourse (2: 1–9) there was danger that the people who had seen the former temple would despise the latter one; and there is need that Haggai should tell them that the glory of this latter house would be greater than the former. This universal shaking of all nations includes convulsions to take place through all the world. It is the convulsion of states and nations which is shown forth, and it is to take place for the glory of God. The people of God were weak. Their enemies were powerful. But the shaking of the world would begin in a little while, and it should be destroyed. After all had been shaken down, God's house should remain. The design for which this is to take place should fill this house with glory. A common interpretation is that "the desire of all nations" (2: 7) is the Messiah. Therefore the meaning would be, that the shaking of all nations would be in order that "the desire of all nations," *i. e.*, the Messiah should come. There are many things attractive in this interpretation, and it coincides well with the result. Still an inspection of the prophet's language in the original will do away with this interpretation. The verb "come" agreeing with "desire of all nations," is in the plural, though the noun "desire" is in the singular, feminine. The agreement, therefore, is in sense and not in letter. "The desire of all nations" is, in the Septuagint, "the most desirable of all nations;" that is, the result will be the conversion of the choicest nations. This is closely allied to the real meaning. "The desire of all nations"—those things that the nations desire—their valuables. It is applied to jewels and other precious objects. The present structure seems mean and poor in comparison with the temple of Solomon, but the prophet tells them that God would shake down all nations till they should lose their

hostility to Him. And they would delight to help Israel to fill the house of God with glory. They should bring their treasures to it, or more probably the glory—the treasures themselves. In order to assure them of His ability to accomplish this, He adds further promises. Consequently at any time He pleases, He can give peace to His people. Upon this interpretation we are not clear to the very letter of the passage. The real temple signifies the spiritual.

3. Third discourse, 2: 10–19. This relates to the first discourse. Everything is vitiated by their former neglect, but God's blessing will attend their reviving zeal.

4. Fourth discourse, 2: 20–23. It is related to the second. The shaking of the heavens and the earth, the overthrow of hostile kingdoms, while Zerubbabel, as the representative of the royal house of David, is chosen and protected.

ZECHARIAH.

Name, parentage, priestly descent, age, beginning of ministry, its duration. Matt. 23: 35. Three parts: 1. Chs. 1–6, series of visions. 2. Chs. 7, 8, answer to a question proposed by the people. 3. Chs. 9–14, prophecies in literal terms relating to future fortunes of God's people. Difficulty in the citation, Matt. 27: 9; various solutions, Zechariah not the author, error in transcription, a peculiar order of the prophets, combined reference to two passages. Genuineness of chs. 9–14; objections; (*a*) style and character; (*b*) incidental allusions, Judah and Israel, 11: 14, or Ephraim, 9: 13; 10: 6, 7; but see 1: 19; 8: 13, Ezek. 37: 16; king of Gaza, 9: 5, Assyria and Egypt, 10: 10, 11; idolatry, 10: 2; 13: 2. No allusion to any king in Judah. Position in this book not explicable otherwise. **Divisions.** I. Chs. 1–6, eight visions. First, 1: 7–17, man on red horse; second, 1: 8–21, four horns and carpenters; third, ch. 2, measuring line; fourth, ch. 3, high-priest in filthy garments; fifth, ch. 4, candlestick and two olive trees; sixth, 5: 1–4, flying roll; seventh, 5: 5–11, woman in an ephah; eighth, 6: 1–8, chariots issuing from between two mountains. Symbolical section, 6: 9–15, the crowned priest. II. Chs. 7, 8, continued observance of fasts; 7: 4–14, rebuke of spirit in which they had been kept; ch. 8, happy future. III. Chs. 9–14, scenes from future fortunes of God's people, from their protection in the time of Alexander to final overthrow of all enemies.

Ch. 9: burden of Hadrach, pledge of protection, vs. 9, 10 in Zion's King, Maccabean deliverance, v. 13. Ch. 11: Desolation of land, vs. 1-3, its predicted cause, vs. 4-14, the treatment of the good shepherd, Beauty and Bands, three shepherds cut off, his price; vs. 15-17, abandoned to foolish shepherd. Chs. 12, 13: Jerusalem assailed, delivered, outpouring of spirit, mourning by families, fountain opened, sin abandoned; judgment to follow the smiting of the shepherd. Ch. 14: Jerusalem besieged by all nations, taken, miraculous rescue, living waters, judgment on gathered foes, universal consecration.

MALACHI.

Name, date, self-righteousness of people (*a*) claiming that they had fulfilled their duty; (*b*) demanding a better recompense. Two parts: I. 1:2; 2:16, their obligations and sins; (*a*) 1:2-5, their obligations to God; (*b*) 1:6; 2:9, sins directly against God; (*c*) 2:10-16, against their brethren. II. 2:17; 4:6, judgment and recompense; (*a*) 2:17; 3:6, severity of the test which the Lord shall apply at his coming; messenger to prepare the way; Angel of the covenant, Christ contemplated not as a redeemer but a judge; (*b*) 3:7-12, their desert of the curse with which they had been visited; (*c*) 3:13; 4:6, distinction to be made between the righteous and the wicked. Elijah; the last of the prophets ends with the announcement of the herald of the new dispensation.

MICAH.

Name, Morasthite, in days of Jotham, Ahaz and Hezekiah. Title disputed, (*a*) from form of prophet's name. But various forms used interchangeably in same passage: and masoretic note to Jer. 26:18 no proof of later usage; (*b*) from subject of prophecy, but see 1:5, 6; (*c*) from Jer. 26:18, but this does not limit his ministry to reign of Hezekiah; (*d*) from contents of book, but disagreement of those who allege it; 4:9, 10 does not refer to carrying away of Manasseh; denial of prophetic foresight.

Summary of prophet's ministry, not distinct discourses. Three sections ch. 1, 2, chs. 3-5, chs. 6, 7. In the first judgment preponderates, and negative side of coming salvation. In the second, mercy, the positive salvation, person of Messiah. In the third, the threatenings justified, and promises appropriated.

THE FULFILMENT OF PROPHECY.

Abridged from Dr. Green's article in Princeton Review, Jan., 1861.

Between prophecy and its fulfilment in history, there can be no discrepancy; but there may be, and there is, a very wide difference in the mode of their representation. Prophecy surveys its objects from its own definite point of view. History sets each in its proper position in respect of time and attendant circumstances.

The prophetic differs from the historical mode of representation chiefly in respect, first, to the time, and second, to the form of the events predicted. Prophecy very commonly neglects the relations of time. It was seldom necessary, in order to the lesson to be drawn from the future events, that anything should be known as to the time of their occurrence, their precise duration, or the intervals which were to separate them. Again, the revelation of time might defeat the design of the lesson itself. The knowledge that a judgment was still far off, might convert it for the present into a temptation to carnal security.

Where any important end was to be answered by it, the time was definitely revealed.

To Abraham, Gen. 15 : 3, the four hundred years of oppression.

To Isaiah, 7 : 8, the sixty-five years within which Ephraim was to cease being a people; also 16 : 14, the three years to the humbling of Moab; 21 : 16, the one year to the reduction of Kedar; 23 : 17, the seventy years of Tyre's depression.

To Jeremiah, 29 : 10, the seventy years of the captivity.

To Habakkuk, 1 : 5, its occurrence in the life-time of his hearers.

To Daniel, 9 : 24–26, the seventy weeks to Messiah's coming.

Sometimes where the precise time was unimportant, some idea of its relative duration was desirable. *Cf.* Ezek. 4 : 5, 6; 29 : 9, 12. In Revelation, the three years and a half of the humiliation of the church, and three days and a half of the triumph of antichrist, and the thousand years of the reign of the saints. All the above Dr. Green cites with a "perhaps."

Relations of time may be disregarded in four ways:

1st. The logical method; when events are grouped agreeably to their affinities or their relation of cause and effect; irrespective of their chronological position. Thus a denunciation of the penalty may immediately follow upon a charge of sin, because they are indissolubly linked together, whatever interval of time may separate them.

Any event in the progress of God's plan of grace may be set in connection with the ultimate result to which it looks, and of which it is a necessary or important antecedent. The curse upon Canaan, Gen. 9: 25, did not enter upon its accomplishment until ages after it had been uttered. The promise to the patriarchs, Gen. 26: 4, was that they should have a numerous posterity, possess the land of their sojournings, and all nations be blessed in them. The salvation of the world is here joined with the multiplication of their descendants and their settlements in Canaan, and there is no intimation that the events may not be simultaneous or immediately successive. Habakkuk, 2: 14, fall of Babylon and the glory of the Lord filling the earth; the destruction of that great oppressing power one of the necessary antecedents to the perfect triumph and universality of the Kingdom of God.

The prophets often present events in classes according to their respective characters. Joel throws together all the evils to be experienced by the chosen people under the symbol of the ravages of locusts; then the blessings they were to experience; and lastly, the judgments upon their foes. Yet these three were intermingled throughout the entire course of history. Cf. Is. 10: 11; 40: 66: Jerem. 33; Messiah and return from Babylon. Zech. 9: 8. 9.

2d. The complex method: events, which occupy long periods in their performance and advance by successive stages, are condensed into a single picture. The characteristic features which it assumes at different periods, belong still to one common subject, and are properly included in its complete delineation. Thus, the fall of a great empire is commonly not accomplished in a moment. The heavy blow which initiates the process of decline may be separated by centuries from the complete ruin. The prophets give to the whole its unity and connection by exhibiting it in a single scene. Isaiah, 13: 17–22 links the capture of Babylon by the Medes with its final and utter desolation; its decline began with the conquest of Cyrus, although it continued for a long time to flourish.

The prophets often link divine judgments upon particular nations with the final judgment upon the whole world; these different acts being but parts of the one continued exercise of his punitive justice. Is. 13: 6-13, fall of Babylon connected with the day of the Lord when the sun and stars shall be darkened and the earth removed out of its place. Mat. 24, destruction of Jerusalem linked with end of the world. Zech. 9: 9, 10, Christ riding upon an ass and reigning from sea to sea; his work in humiliation and exaltation, being viewed in its totality. Cf. Joel, 2: 28-32, the beginning and end of the Messianic period is presented in its unity.

3d. The apotelesmatic method; the last of a long series of events is described to the exclusion of the others, in order to exhibit the matter in its mature form. As the political philosopher often neglects to describe a constitution in its earlier and undeveloped form, speaking of it only in its completion; so the prophets most frequently present the Kingdom of Christ in its triumph and glory. It is to be judged by what it shall be when all opposition is vanquished, and it is allowed, without restraint or foreign commixture, to put on its own proper form, and to reveal its true nature. Is. 11, rod of Jesse immediately followed by the wolf dwelling with the lamb. Cf. Dan. 2: 44.

4th. The generic method; predictions are made, not of an individual event, but of a series, in each of which they have a separate fulfilment. They are commonly such as reveal a principle in the divine administration, which secures a fixed result from given antecedents; as often as the conditions exist, so often will the predicted consequence follow. Jesus announced this rule, Matt. 24: 28.

Deut. 4: 25, ff, transgression to be punished at the hands of the heathen, and mercy to follow repentance; again and again fulfilled. So, too, Is. 40: 3, "voice crying, prepare the way of the Lord." So, too, outpouring of the Spirit, Joel, 2: 28.

Three varieties of the generic prophecy:

(1.) One event, as being important or most fully realizing the common idea, is alone described. Deut. 18: 18, the expressions employed are applicable to all the prophets, but find their highest application in Christ.

(2.) No one of the events exactly represented, but individual traits borrowed from many in the series and blended.

2 Sam. 7 : 12-16, the perpetual royalty of David's seed includes all his descendants who sat upon the theocratic throne, and also Christ. Some of the expressions are conformed to one, others to another of the subjects to which it was intended to apply. In the later prophecies of Isaiah, "the servant of the Lord" applies to the chosen people and to the Redeemer; they had the common commission to perpetuate and spread the true religion. Israel had a part in these predictions, for his name is given to this "servant," 49 : 3; and he is charged with unfaithfulness, 42 : 19. Yet the title belongs in its high sense only to the Messiah, for the vicarious atonement as ascribed to him, 53. The fulfilment by Israel falls within the prediction, but the work of the Messiah is coincident with it.

No mystical or hidden sense is in the words, the same fact or principle, which is represented in the one, appears likewise, but in greater perfection in the other. One of the events may even be past. Thus the Messianic psalms have a partial application to experiences of David and Solomon, or, as in Ps. 8, to man in general; but the terms employed would be extravagant, if nothing more was intended by them. The only adequate explanation is their additional reference to Christ.

(3.) The prophecy may be restricted to what is common to all the events.

A generic element is more or less involved in all prophecies. The facts may not occur again in the precise form; but the laws are permanent, and will have other exemplifications. This explains why later prophets, in adopting the language of their predecessors, not unfrequently make a new application of it. Jer. 48 : 43, 44, about Moab, quoting what Is. 24 : 17, 18, had said of the whole earth. Also Jer. 11 : 19, with Is. 53 : 7. Nahum 1 : 15, with Is. 52 : 7. Revelation resumes the ancient prophecies concerning Babylon.

Prophecy may also depart from the strictly historical form.

In this the same two-fold design as in the neglect of time; viz., the partial obscuring of the events revealed, and the greater distinctness and force of the lessons conveyed.

Had God seen best, he might have revealed the details. He often did so. Cyrus predicted by name, Is. 44 : 28; likewise Josiah, I Kings, 13 : 2. The birth of Christ of a virgin at Bethlehem, &c.

Two methods adopted.
1st. The identity of the object predicted is retained with a mere diversity of form. The future object is spoken of, not as it shall actually be at the time of its fulfilment, but as it is at the time of the prediction. It was spoken of as the people know it, being thus more intelligible to them.

Thus, objects common to the two dispensations are, as a rule, called by their O. T. names and presented in their O. T. form. God's people constantly called Israel their habitation; Canaan, the seat of God's worship or his dwelling place; Jerusalem, Zion of the temple. The conversion of the heathen is represented by their erecting altars in their land and engaging in the ritual worship, Is. 19:19; offering incense and oblations in every place, Mal. 1:11; keeping feast of Tabernacles, Zech. 14:16; paying annual or even monthly and weekly visits to Jerusalem, Is. 66:23; and enrolled amongst the Levitical priesthood, Is. 66:21; although at the time to which these predictions refer, this particular mode of worship would be abolished.

The outpouring of the Spirit, Joel 2:28, is described under the form of speaking with tongues, though sanctification was the universal manifestation.

Names of nations, hostile to the Kingdom of God, are used to those in whom this hostility is perpetuated. Joel, 3:19, Egypt and Edom. Cf. Mic. 5:5, 6; Is. 11:14.

Unity of the people under Messiah is represented by the healing of the breach between Judah and Israel, Is. 11:13; Jer. 3:18. Messiah to sit on David's throne, Is. 9:7. Cf. Ezek. 34:23, Hos. 3:5. We of to-day constantly use the words Canaan, Israel, Zion.

The statements, however, are not false nor inaccurate; simply there is no disclosure made of the changes to be effected in the plan of grace. Even so everything is not made known to us now that is to be revealed hereafter. We have glimpses of but cannot imagine precisely the future. From the glimpses given to the prophets of the future, they invariably return to the representation of the future under forms then existing. Isaiah connects with the new heaven and the new earth, 65:17, building houses and inhabiting them, planting vineyards and eating the fruit, 66:22. Cf. Joel, 3:17; Zech. 14:16.

The literalists maintain that the predictions respecting Israel, Jerusalem and Canaan, in the days of the Messiah and the establishment of his Kingdom in Zion, are to have a national and local fulfilment. They should

1. Remember the principle underlying the whole matter, which is far more comprehensive than the particular cases in dispute.

2. Interpret all prophecies consistently and upon some settled method.

2nd. Another similar object may by a figure be substituted for it. This may be a figure of speech or symbol. Is. 2: 2 "Mentioned of Lord's house . . . . . shall be exalted above the hills;" in strict sense of words, a physical change, but doubtless a moral change of analogous nature is intended.

In the symbolical prophecy, one thing not merely illustrates another, but is substituted for it. The symbol may be

a. Presented to the senses. Zech. 6: 11, the high priest Joshua, crowned with silver and gold brought from Babylon, symbolizes Messiah as both priest and king, to whom all in distant lands should lend their aid. The symbolical action of the prophets are instances of the same kind.

b. Exhibited in vision or dream. The temple and its worship, Ezek. 40; the image of Nebuchadnezzar's dream, Dan. 2, symbolical of the future state of the theocracy. Cf. Dan. 8, Zech. 1.

c. Simply described, and thus partake of the nature of allegory. The locusts, Joel, 1: 2, represent the foes of the covenant people. Cf. Hos. 1: 3; Ezek. 17: 23.

Aids in interpreting symbolical prophecies are three:

(1.) The prominent qualities and associations. Symbols in the Scriptures not like letters of the alphabet, arbitrary and with no resemblance between the sign and the thing signified. The locusts, Joel, 1: 2, are a natural emblem of foreign invaders; filthy garments, Zech. 3: 4, of sin; crowns, Zech. 6: 11, of royalty.

(2.) Established usage. Symbols must have a uniform signification, if they are to be an intelligible medium of communicating ideas.

Some interpret the brazen serpent as a healer, and refer to the serpent in Egyptian symbolism, where it denotes healing, and to its use in the worship of Æsculapius. It is more natural, however, to conclude that either the serpent form in Num. 2: 8, is not symbolical; or else that it retains its constant signification of destroyer (Cf. Rev. 12: 9; 20;

2; and Gen. 3), and, being transfixed and harmless, indicates a victory over the destroyer.

Many symbols borrowed from the Levitical institutions; being familiar, sacred and significant of the very truths with which prophecy was concerned. The signification, belonging to them in their original connection, is always retained. Cherubim, Ezek. 1, and temple, 40.

If the symbol be not illustrated by scriptural usage, we should consider the symbolical use of the same object among other ancient nations, especially those with which Israel was brought into contact.

(3) Authoritative explanation furnished by inspiration sometimes given by the prophet himself. Daniel states the symbol and adds the interpretation of Neb.'s dream, 2.

Sometimes by a letter writer of scripture. "Son of man," Dan. 7: 13, is applied by Christ to himself. The little horn of Daniel's fourth beast, 7, with 2 Thes. 2: 3.

Sometimes the explanation is indirectly given by mingling literal language with the description of the symbol. Cf. Zech. 3: 1.

Distinguish Prophecies.—To distinguish prophecies which adhere to the historical form from those in which it is neglected, the following suggestions suffice:

1. In prophecies already accomplished, the criterion is to be found in the fulfilment. That Christ should rise from the dead without seeing corruption, Ps. 16: 10; that his garments should be parted, &c., Ps. 22: 18, are shown by the event to have been literally intended. The drying up of the river of Egypt, Is. 19: 5, coming of Elijah, Mal. 4: 5, are shown to have been figurative. Perhaps, however, the prophecy has as yet been but partially fulfilled and what was only figuratively true of the past may come to pass literally in the future, Is. 13: 10.

2. Comparison with other prophecies in the O. or N. T. relating to the same subject, is valuable. The figures of one may be detected by the literal language of another, or by the figures of another with which they would be incompatible if literally understood.

Heathen, when converted, build altars, and offer sacrifices in their own land, Is. 19: 19–21; and that in all parts of the earth, Mal. 1: 11. Yet they are said to go up to Jerusalem to worship, Is. 2: 3.

Cf. Joel, 3: 18 with Ezek. 47: 1, Zech. 14: 8.
Cf. Ezek. 38: 2 with Rev. 20: 8.

3. N. T. teaches that the restrictions of the old economy and its ceremonial are now abolished. Consequently, if any prediction speaks of these obselete forms in connection with Messianic times, it must be understood, not according to its letter, but according to its spirit. See Gal. 4 : 9; Acts 15 : 10; Heb. 10 : 1, 2; John 4 : 21; Eph. 2 : 14.

4. The figurative character of a prophecy is often stated or suggested. Ezek. 37 : 11, declares the resurrection of the dry bones to mean the restoration of Israel. Also, Dan. 7 : 8; Joel, 2 : 4, 5, 20; Zech. 10 : 11; Jer. 25 : 15.

5. When the terms of a prediction stand in evident relation to the past history of the chosen people, or to typical events and institutions, there is reason to suspect that these may be figuratively employed

Thus a second dividing of the Red Sea, Is. 11 : 15.

See, also, Ezek. 20 : 34–38, Is. 48 : 21, Ezek. 38 : 22, Is. 11 : 6–8, 65 : 25.

6. If the literal explanation would involve a physical impossibility, or a manifest incongruity, this is a clear index of the figurative character of a prediction.

Ezek. 42 : 16, a temple of this size could not be placed upon Mt. Moriah. See, also, Rev. 21 : 16, Joel, 2 : 20, Ezek. 39 : 12.

7. The general literary style of a prophet affords a hint as to the character of a particular passage in his writings.

8. In prophecies yet unfulfilled, the developments of Providence must decide. It could not have been known in advance that the prophetic appellations, Josiah, 1 K. 13 : 2, and Cyrus, Is. 45 : 1, 4, were to be real names; and that Immanuel, Is. 7 : 14, was not. See, also, Mal. 4 : 5.

9. The line between figurative and literal prophecies is not to be too sharply drawn, as though these formed quite distinct classes. The same prophecy may be intended and fulfilled in both senses. Opening the eyes of the blind and the ears of the deaf, Is. 35 : 5, was fulfilled literally in the miracles of Christ and figuratively in the blessings of the gospel dispensation. See, also, Hag. 2 : 7–9, Zech. 9 : 9.

The literal fulfillment sometimes serves to identify the subject of the figurative. That John came preaching in the wilderness of Judea, was an external sign that he was the voice spoken of by Isaiah as crying in the spiritual wilderness, "Prepare." John 19 : 36, a literal mark of similitude, identifies Christ as the true paschal lamb.

The study of a prophecy is for the purpose of drawing therefrom instruction, and is therefore quite distinct from the study of its fulfillment. As to the latter, two directions are important.

Fulfillment of Prophecy.—1. It should be preceded by a thorough study of the prophecy itself. The reversion of this order has led to the most extravagant results. Some of the old Dutch interpreters found in the O. T. prophecies all the events of the Thirty Years' War.

2. The student should proceed from the plain to the obscure, from the fulfilled to the unfulfilled. When engaged upon prophecies which are clear, or where the fulfillment is before his eyes, the student is in less danger of error, and may correct his result by the divine exposition afforded by the event. Having thus tested and adjusted his methods, he may adventure prudently and cautiously into those whose fulfillment is still future.

Uses of the study of the fulfillment of prophecy.

1st. Practical; it sheds light upon duty and the incentives to its faithful performance. We learn also the nature of the events which are transpiring around us and their place in the divine plan. Thus the early Christians anticipated the destruction of Jerusalem and made good their escape.

2nd. Apologetic; there is no clearer proof of Divinity than infallible foreknowledge of the distant and contingent future. There are so many plain prophecies that the strength of the argument could not be increased by the addition of more.

Actual Fulfillment.—To the question, whether all the prophecies of Scripture have been or are to be fulfilled, a negative answer has been returned by two very different classes of interpreters, and on essentially different grounds. Many believers in the inspiration of the prophets have contended that certain prophecies contain implied conditions upon which their fulfillment or non-fulfillment, according to the tenor of their announcement, is suspended. The Socinians held it to be inconsistent with the liberty of free agents that their acts should be foreknown or certainly determined beforehand; all predictions relating to the free acts of men must, consequently, upon this theory, be contingent or conditional. The schoolmen distinguish three sorts of prophecies — *prophetia prædestionationis*, *prophetia præscientiæ* and *prophetia comminationis*. The prophecy of predestination is when the event depends wholly upon God's will, without any respect to the will of man, as the prophecy of the incarnation of Christ; the prophecy of prescience is of such things as depend upon the liberty of man's will; and the prophecy of commination denotes God's denunciations of heavy judgments against a people. The first and second rest upon the Divine decree and foreknowledge, and they always take effect; the third is a simple declaration of what is deserved, and, in the existing state of things, is to be expected, but which need not follow if the antecedent conditions are altered.

The decisive objection to this view, on whatever footing it is placed, or by whatever grounds it is defended, is that the inspired criterion for distinguishing true from false prophets, is the accomplishment of their predictions, Deut. xviii. 22. This test would be practically rendered nugatory if predictions of specific events, expressed in absolute terms and with no intimation of any condition, might fail of fulfilment, and yet be true prophecies. And that Jeremiah xviii. 7-10, had no intention of nullifying this test, appears from his appeal to it in his contest with Hananiah, Jer. xxviii. 9. The righteous dispensations of God towards men are indeed conditioned by their character and conduct, so that a change in them is followed by a change in his dealings with them, which the Scriptures, employing the language of men and speaking according to the outward appearance, often described as a change in the Divine mind. But God's eternal purpose never changes. His foresight of the future is not conditional, but absolute, and he may, if he pleases, reveal it absolutely. When a specific good is unconditionally promised, therefore, it is because it is certain to the divine mind that his mercy will not be taken away from the object of his favor. When a specific evil is similarly threatened, it is with the certainty that they who are thus doomed are incorrigible and will not repent. Even where this is the case, as in Isa. vi. 9, etc., the prophecy is not useless, as Fairbairn objects. It still serves two important purposes. It is a witness on God's behalf and against the obdurate offenders, that judgment did not come upon them without just cause, or without antecedent warning; and it may be the means of leading individuals to repentance and salvation, though the unbelieving mass persist in going on to ruin. There may be no claim upon God, *ab extra*, to fulfil his threatenings, but the reasons of his acts are in himself, and his inviolable truth and justice stand in the way of his revoking them. Whenever the moral effect of a prophecy required that it should be conditional, it is made so in express terms. Or, the same end may be answered by leaving it indefinite, announcing some general principle of the Divine administration, without specifying when or how it shall go into effect, or, at least, leaving the time undetermined. But whatever is absolutely declared by the prophet, is to be absolutely understood. The most plausible exception is that derived from the case of Jonah. Nineveh continued to stand, notwithstanding his having been sent of God with the declaration, "Yet forty days and Nineveh shall be overthrown." But, as Hengstenberg has well said, we have only this general statement respecting Jonah's preaching there, not the preaching itself. No doubt this was such as to indicate the only hope of escape lay in a timely repentance. It was, at least, so understood by the Ninevites, and they acted accordingly. Jonah's displeasure at the sparing of the city cannot be urged in proof of the unconditional character of his prophecy; for there is reason to believe that this did not arise from the fear of his being discredited as a prophet, but rather from his distress at seeing the mercy of God transferred from obdurate Israel to their penitent foes. Jer. 26 : 18, 19, to which Caspari* appeals in proof of the conditional character of Micah's prophecy, iii. 12, is still less to the point. It simply repeats the opinion of certain elders, without vouching for its correctness. The prediction in question relates to an event whose time was not defined by the prophet, although intimated, iv. 10, and it was fulfilled to the letter.

On the other hand, unbelievers in the inspiration of the prophets allege that several of their predictions failed of accomplishment, thereby showing that they had no certain knowledge of the future. Thus De Wette:† "Jer. xxii. 18, etc., xxxvi. 30, appear not to have been fulfilled, comp. 2 Kings xxiv. 6; 2 Chron. xxxvi. 6. The following are not fulfilled: Amos vii. 11; Hosea ix. 3, xi. 5; Isa. xxii., xxix., xvi. 14; xxiii.; Jer. xliii. 8, etc., xlix. 7, etc.; Ezek. xxxv.,

---

* Caspari on Micah, p. 160.

† Einleitung in die A. T. § 204. In the translation of this work by Theodore Parker, the translator has mistaken his author's meaning, when he makes him say, "The definite predictions of Ezekiel xii. xxiv. 25, 26, xxxiii. 21, 22, seem not to have been fulfilled." De Wette merely alleges these as instances of the prediction of specific events, without denying their fulfilment, this being too plain to be questioned.

xxix., xxxviii , etc.; not accurately fulfilled, Isa. vii 17, etc., viii. 4, xiv. 23, xvii. 1-3, xxxiv. 9, etc." But even if we were not able to prove that these particular prophecies have been accomplished, this would not affect the argument of inspiration from the remainder, many of which have been most signally and undeniably fulfilled. This is sufficient, likewise, to show that we should be slow to admit the non-fulfillment of any prophecy uttered by those who are so clearly attested as the messengers of God. Nothing but the plainest and most undeniable evidence can justify such an admission. But so far from this being afforded, an examination of the passages adduced by De Wette, will show that his denial rests in every case upon a false interpretation of the passages themselves, a want of historical knowledge, or the groundless assumption that the prophecies contemplate only the immediate future. Amos vii. 11, 'Jeroboam shall die by the sword,' is not the language of Amos, but words which Amaziah slanderously puts into his mouth, to make him odious to the king. The real words of Amos were, vii. 9, " I will rise against the *house* of Jeroboam with the sword," which came to pass, 2 Kings xv. 10. Ezekiel's prophecy respecting Gog, chaps. xxxviii., xxxix., relates to events still future. Isaiah, ch. xxxiv., blends the final judgment with the judgment upon Edom. Isa. vii. 17, the invasion of Judah by the king of Assyria; Isa. xiv. 23, the utter desolation of Babylon; and Jer. xlix. 7, etc.; Ezek. ch. xxxv., that of Edom, have been fulfilled to the letter, and the length of time which intervened between the predictions and their accomplishment, only enhances the evidence of prophetic foresight. According to 2 Kings xv. 29, xvi. 9, the riches of Damascus and the spoil of Samaria (not the city, but the kingdom) were taken away before the king of Assyria within the time predicted, Isa. viii. 4. That Damascus was in consequence temporarily desolated Isa. xvii. 1-3, is as credible as the desolation of Samaria and Jerusalem in their respective captivities. In regard to Isa. xvi. 14, the overthrow of Moab within three years, Isa. xxiii., the humiliation of Tyre for seventy years, and its subsequent revival, and Jer. xliii. 8, etc., Ezek. xxix., Nebuchadnezzar's subjugation of Egypt, the sole difficulty arises from the deficiency of historical records. We know nothing of Moab's history, except from the incidental references occasionally made to it in the Old Testament. But it was, in all probability, devastated by the Assyrian armies, which so often invaded Palestine. It is well known that Tyre was besieged by Nebuchadnezzar for thirteen years, and there is good reason to believe successfully, although the fact of its capture does not happen to be mentioned in express terms. It cannot, at any rate, be disproved; neither can his conquest of Egypt, which is, moreover, asserted by Josephus, *Antiquities*, x. 9, 7, who quotes Megasthenes and Berosus to the same effect, *Antiquities*, x. 11, 1. These positive statements are certainly sufficient to outweigh the silence of Herodotus and Diodorus. The indignities threatened to the dead body of Jehoiakim, Jer. xxii. 18, etc., xxxvi. 30, are not discredited by 2 Kings xxiv. 6, 2 Chron. xxxvi. 6, for there is no conflict between these passages and the prophecy. Nor is there any reason to question Josephus' explicit testimony to its fulfilment, *Antiq*. x. 6, 3, notwithstanding its rejection by De Wette. The difficulty in Isa. xxii. 29, is not so much to discover a fulfilment, as to decide between different events which have a claim to be so regarded. The invasion of Sennacherib seems to have been more immediately regarded in both cases. Elam and Kir, chap. xxii. 5, denote troops from those nations in the Assyrian army; and the sudden and miraculous defeat, xxix. 5, etc., is that of the host of the Assyrians. But with this is blended the foresight, in chap. xxix, of other trials and deliverances; and perhaps, in chap. xxii., of the later sieges by Esar-haddon and Nebuchadnezzar. Hos. ix. 3, "Ephraim shall return to Egypt," and xi. 5, "he shall not return into the land of Egypt, but the Assyrian shall be his king," are mutually contradictory, if regard be had merely to the letter and the form of expression. In thus affirming and denying the same proposition, the prophet must, if he is to be absolved from the charge of inconsistency, have intended it in different senses. Two explanations are possible, either of which is satisfactory. He may mean, Ephraim shall return to an Egypt, *i. e*, he shall be reduced again to a servitude like that which he formerly experienced in that land—not in the literal Egypt, however, but in Assyria. Or he may mean some of the people shall return to Egypt, fugitives from Assyrian invasion; the mass, however, shall be carried not to Egypt, but to Assyria. Upon either of these hypotheses, the language of the prediction accords with the event. And these explanations will still hold good, though xi. 5 be translated with De Wette, interrogatively, Shall he not return into the land of Egypt? There is no note of interrogation in the Hebrew, however, so that the declarative form, adopted in the common English version, is to be preferred.

www.ingramcontent.com/pod-product-compliance
Lightning Source LLC
Chambersburg PA
CBHW022013220426
43663CB00007B/1060